ESCAPING CHURCH

A Guide to Life Outside the Institution

TIM MATHER

BCR Press

DEDICATION

To Pleasant Katie: Who knew?

TABLE OF CONTENTS

Preface

COACHING

The gifting in which I operate within the ranks of the Saints may best be described as coaching. The motivation behind coaching is not to usurp the place of the player, but to serve as eyes into his blind spots and a resource providing data he may not perceive on his own. Its purpose is to help the player achieve greatness.

Coaches are not perfect; nonetheless, we all need them. Tiger Woods is perhaps the greatest golfer of all time, yet he continues to submit his play to several coaches who will never play as well as he. Tiger knows that they understand the game and the pitfalls inherent to it; he knows their insight makes him better. They have studied his swing and can pinpoint a problem when something goes wrong.

The purpose of this book is to provide coaching on the basics of the adventure upon which so many of us have embarked outside of the traditional church setting.

If you have ever played a sport you know that coaches are usually pretty strong with their instruction. Their adamancy is intended to make the player better, to improve his skills, providing insight into weak areas and enhancing his strengths. You will find many forceful statements in these pages which, depending upon your vantage point, might be interpreted as anger or arrogance. Be assured, the arguments made herein are gleaned not only from my own experience, but also from the experiences of many hundreds of friends with whom we have walked these many years. So do not mistake adamancy for anger. It is vital that you consider these recommendations—because that is all they are: recommendations—as possible help on your journey. If you tend to be easily offended, you will have many opportunities to be upset by what is said or how it is said. Only know this: my intention is to sharpen your skills and your mental acuity for the adventure.

The road ahead is treacherous—at times it disappears altogether—but the adventure is well worth the effort.

Chapter 1

A Coach's Notes

Recycled Salt

She couldn't help it; she just *had* to look back. And there it was: everything she had ever known, every place she had ever felt comfortable; all that she understood about life was right there over her shoulder.

Wherever her husband Lot was running, it was most certainly toward something unknown—after all Sodom represented our way of thinking, our very existence depended upon a nice, cozy understanding of how the world of Sodom worked—and this journey *away* was just crazy.

The urge to look back was not just rebellion against what the angel had instructed; it represented a yearning for the good old days, for the familiar. He'd specifically told us not to do it, but she decided that a quick look wouldn't hurt anything. So she looked back. Her eyes focused upon the thing she had left behind, and she was transformed by the sight of it... transformed into a pillar of salt.

Salt is a dichotomy. Life cannot exist without it. Yet, when too much of it is piled in one place, the area surrounding it dies. Anyone who faithfully throws down salt on the driveway to melt ice will testify that when spring comes, the grass along the driveway is always dead.

But who can eat scrambled eggs without a little salt? Without it they taste sort of like wet dryer lint. Salt transforms the mundane into tasty delights, and it is used to preserve the essentials of life. During double sessions at the beginning of the football season,

we were urged to swallow salt pills so that we wouldn't have a legitimate excuse for the utter exhaustion riding down upon us like the four horsemen of the apocalypse. The human body cannot exist without salt, and yet, when old age makes its appearance (sagging skin and all) that extra shake of salt can cause our blood pressure to rise until it feels like the top of our head will blow right off.

Jesus used salt as a metaphor for the Saints—preserving, bringing seasoning to the planet—and warned us that it is possible to miss our mission by losing our saltiness, thus leaving the world without seasoning.

The best thing to hit the traditional church in the past two thousand years is the Great Escape going on right now. The church has spent all of its time looking back and singing, "Gimme that ol' time religion" unaware that our saltiness is gone. So the salt crystals are escaping, leaving the pillar of salt that the church has become with its dead traditions and liturgies; and they are discovering how to season their own families, their neighbors, and one another like something not seen since the first dispersion. When it first happened in Acts 11, the Good News had left a static pillar of salt in Jerusalem but Father flung them throughout the known world resulting in unprecedented growth of the Kingdom of heaven on earth.

Having escaped the destruction of the sinful world, the institutional church has, in slow motion over the centuries, looked back and has been transformed into a pillar of salt, unmovable in its theology and tradition, deadly to everything around it, and without any seasoning influence upon society. Father has allowed us a couple thousand years of pillar building, but now He is crushing these pillars to man's religious stagnation and is flinging us back into the culture to preserve it from decay and destruction.

He's all done with pillars; this is the day of *"two or three gathered together"* to bring delight rather than the thousands huddling together under our church-growth banner while ignoring the death it perpetuates around us.

But without the rest of the pillar—we've been duped into believing that growing our pillar is Father's plan—we may feel out of sorts and alone. What follows is a guide for the journey ahead as you escape the pillar and once again season the world around you.

WHAT ARE WE NOT DOING?

The traditional church is what it is. I am neither angry at it nor do I think I am tasked with destroying it. The church, for better or worse, is Jesus' problem. However, the traditional view of the church will be adamantly challenged herein to point out how you have been negatively educated concerning your spiritual life.

Before launching into a description of what this guide is, it is vital that you gain an understanding of what it is *not*. Most importantly, it is not an attempt on my part to command, plead, urge, cajole, or otherwise lure the reader out of the institutional church. Additionally, this book is not in any way advocating the angry, accusatory tone of many who have left the traditional church system, only to be trapped in the jaws of condemnation toward the institution itself or toward those who remain within its grasp. If you find yourself outside the doors of the church, then this guide is for you. However, it is for your *freedom*, not for adding ammunition to some hateful, malicious assault upon the traditional church. Everyone knows the church has problems.

Your ranting helps no one; your hurt must be healed; you must let it go and move on. Some tools toward healing from spiritual abuse may be found within these pages along with instruction as to the path to real wholeness. Lay down the hurt, the anger, and the accusations for your own sake and for the sake of Jesus, who, by the way, bore it all for you already.

SOME FRESH LANGUAGE

There is some confusion with much of the language used in the traditional church structure. Some words are over-used while meanings of other words have evolved inappropriately. Therefore, let's clarify what a few words will mean in the pages to follow.

The Called Out Ones

It is my contention that the word "church" has been so totally corrupted in the excesses and perversions of the traditional church structure that it should be eliminated from our vocabulary in favor of the actual definition of the word. The Greek word "ecclesia" translated "church" in English Bibles actually means "Called Out Ones." Everyone who has been saved more than fifteen minutes has heard some preacher say those words: "The building is not the church; we are the church." Yet everything the institution does—its meetings, its programs, its liturgy—centers around the building, therefore, without that edifice, there can be no "church." *"Let us not give up meeting together"* (Hebrews 10:25) is the trumpet call to come to the church building. Supposedly, if you don't come to the building, then you are either backslidden or in rebellion. Why can't *"meeting together"* simply mean getting together at the coffee shop or at work or on your back deck?

Therefore, we will identify those who have been cleansed

by the Blood of the Lamb of God, saved, born again, born from above, redeemed, or otherwise confessed their sins and now walk with Jesus, as the Called Out Ones. It will be used interchangeably with the term Saints, since that is what the Called Out Ones are.

The corrupted English word "church" will be used hereafter to identify the "institution," the traditional Protestant or Catholic Church, church buildings, and denominations. Church is wrongly something one *does* or one *attends* as opposed to its real meaning: some*one*. Since the word has lost its pure meaning in the common vernacular, "church" will only be used in this negative context.

Throughout the text you will find the phrases "institution," traditional church," or "church system," used interchangeably to identify the common view of church: a building, a denomination, or an organization of people meeting under a pastor or leader who teaches or preaches in a lecture style. Unfortunately, you may find its use to appear entirely negative. You will see that by using it in this way, I am not attacking people but the subjugation by an organization in which they voluntarily participate.

The word "church" does not define an organization or a building. It indicates *people*. Though groups of Called Out Ones may come together to worship or fellowship; they are not more the church when they gather than when they are alone. You are as much the "church," a Called Out One, when you are in the shower or standing in line at the grocery store as when you are sitting in a pew.

Basic Church

The phrase "basic church" conveys the biblical concept of what a gathering of Saints should include. It is taken from one of the only sections of the New Testament that give clues as to what we should do.

*When you come together, everyone has a hymn,
or a word of instruction, a revelation, a tongue or
an interpretation. All of these must be done for the
strengthening of the church.*
1 Corinthians 14:26

Therefore, when we get together to fellowship, everyone who comes should bring something to share with the others. Bring something out of your own spiritual journey that will encourage, instruct, or bless the friends with whom you gather.

The atmosphere of a basic gathering is casual, as a family might gather. This is in direct opposition to what we know to be a "meeting." We will use "basic church" to distinguish it from other adaptations springing up across the world. Many institutional churches develop cell groups as a nod to the necessity of the Called Out Ones meeting in homes or offices or schools, but this is a far cry from where Father is going. In fact, some cell groups may just be the biggest hindrance to realizing one's full Called-Out-One potential since the authority remains centralized within the institution.

Escapee

We will use this descriptive term to indicate those who, by their own volition, have left, or are in the process of leaving the traditional church. They will have attempted to escape the buildings and the paradigms of the institution. They are, therefore, Escapees.

Spectator

The traditional church system is designed for one person to do ministry at a time while the rest of the group watches. The term Spectator will be used herein to indicate what might otherwise be called church people, pew warmers, church members, i.e., the laity. They simply *watch*.

14

THE ADVENTURE BEGINS

Although our own story is used from time to time, the purpose of this text is not to use our experience as a model for everyone else. You will find stories of other adventurers whose journeys are quite divergent from our own. Our hope is that you will find Father's way for you.

As we begin this adventure together please recognize one final truth: we have learned what is found within these pages through a series of dreadful mistakes, plenty of confusion, and much bungling through the darkness, not knowing where we were or where we were going. Hopefully, we can help you avoid some of the same gaffes by pointing out some of the pitfalls as well as some of the joys of this new life outside the institution.

COACH'S TIP

It is time to move from Spectator
to full-grown, mature Called Out One.
It will be at once thrilling and terrifying.
Keep your chin up; it gets better.

"Continue to work out your salvation with fear and trembling, for it is God who works in you to will and to act according to his good purpose."
Philippians 2:12b-13

Chapter 2

WHERE ARE WE GOING?

FATHER'S KIDS

God's people are God's people no matter where they find themselves, whether they are in prison, in the corporate world, in a hut somewhere in a Third World country, standing in an ancient cathedral, or sitting across the table from friends in a house. We are still His kids, and nothing, *"neither death nor life, neither angels nor demons, neither the present nor the future, nor any powers, neither height nor depth, nor anything else in all creation, will be able to separate us from the love of God that is in Christ Jesus our Lord"* (Romans 8:38-39).

Nothing… despite the exhaustive efforts of popes, bishops, kings, presidents, senators, Imams, priests, husbands, wives, parents, children… and pastors.

Even though this text focuses upon the challenges of Escapees who have left the traditional church, many of those who are still within the walls of the institution are God's people as well. We make no value judgments against those who decide to stay in church. However, the choices someone makes concerning those church structures, models, or traditions crafts a distinctly different destiny as to the levels of freedom and liberty in which they may be able to live.

Spiritual Prison

Egypt was at first a place of salvation for the children of Israel. They fled there during a fierce famine and it became the place of safety for the entire family. They lived for a time within the security of its borders and enjoyed relative peace. But as is always the case for God's people, staying in one place for an extended period of time soon changed it from salvation to bondage. They found themselves enslaved by the upper class of the land, forced to do their bidding under the crack of a whip. The oppression increased over time until it became unbearable.

Something had to change.

Father, in His mercy, sent a deliverer to lead them from bondage to the Promised Land, a land flowing with milk and honey. The departure was traumatic, the journey treacherous, but off they went in obedience to His call.

Egypt, in this model, does not represent sin because they were already the Children of God. It represents the progression from freedom to bondage to freedom that many are experiencing as they escape the cruelty of the traditional church system and set out on the journey to their Promised Land. At one time the church was the place of salvation for many of us. There we discovered the presence of God who satisfied our hunger. We grew in the faith there—to one extent or another—and found relative peace.

Yet, over time, this place of salvation became a place of bondage. We are reminded of the Galatian brothers and sisters who were chided by Paul: *"I am astonished that you are so quickly deserting the one who called you by the grace of Christ and are turning to a different gospel"* (Galatians 1:6). The Good News we received has been somehow changed from *"Now the Lord is the Spirit, and where the Spirit of the Lord is, there is freedom"* (2 Corinthians 3:17), to a preacher's directive to "watch me do my calling." Is that really the definition of freedom?

There is *more*.

I view my time in the pastorate as prison ministry. Just as Egypt became Israel's prison, so the institutional church system has become a place of captivity. It is dear to Father's heart to care for those in prison, even if they invented the prison themselves. God's people are still his people no matter what chains they endure. As a pastor, I was imprisoned just like my parishioners. I was like a prison trustee since I was performing some marginally useful tasks within the institution. The churches that I served grew and people came to Christ, but there was always something in the back of my mind haunting me. I secretly wondered, "Is this really what Jesus had in mind when He died for us?"

I had to come to terms with the fact that, in my ignorance, I perpetuated the prison system. I grew up in the church; I was schooled and trained to lead it; I accepted my chains because the system said it was the only way to fulfill the call of God upon my life.

THE EXODUS

In 1993, I was fasting and praying to hear some direction from the Lord for my personal walk and for the church. What I heard changed my life forever. The Holy Spirit spoke to my heart, "Preaching, in its present form, nauseates me." I wrote it down, horrified. For years I had said, "I merely exist for six days and twenty-three hours every week just to do the one thing I was born to do: preaching."

Father floored me with His statement. I went through the process of testing the prophetic word. I knew it wasn't me; I loved preaching. Why would it be the Enemy? Of course preaching nauseates him: it reaches the lost for Jesus. He wouldn't say something so obvious.

I knew it was Father.

In the weeks following that encounter, I had the most

18

powerful vision of my life. I share it with you now to reveal my heart for you as you make this transition. Here is the vision I call "Dragging Out the Dead."

As I looked, I could see the backs of a large crowd of people to my left. They were intently looking in the same direction away from me. It was obvious they were engaged in worship—some with hands raised, some with bowed heads, most were singing. I watched myself disappear into the crowd and reappear dragging a dead person by the collar. I dragged the person across the street and laid him on his back with his head against the curb. I continued to enter and reappear with more dead people until there was a long line of bodies lying side by side along the curb.

All at once, I began to weep over them because they were dead. Then, I walked out before them, raised my hands and spoke over them. I could not hear what was said, but immediately, they all sat up. For the next few minutes, they began to recover and make their way, one by one, to a standing position. It took some longer than others, but eventually, they were all standing.

As their recovery process was proceeding, I disappeared once again into the throng and began dragging more dead people out. When those from the first group were able to stand and then walk, they joined me in dragging out more and more bodies. Each time the area along the curb was full, I stepped forward, raised my arms and spoke. The whole line of bodies would sit up alive, make their way to a standing position, and eventually help us in our work.

Before long, my view began to pan back to see the extent of the crowd worshiping off to my left. There were hundreds of thousands, maybe even millions, gathered around a circular object in the middle. This object was domed at its center and was turning around very slowly, much like a merry-go-round. It radiated a bright light that the people worshiped. At the center of the object stood a brilliant angel with his arms outstretched receiving the adoration of the crowd. The people were worshiping the angel in a myriad of styles and traditions, from the solemn to the exuberant. As I looked closer, the Holy Spirit opened my eyes to see that the angel was not an angel of light after all but a dark angel appearing as an angel of light. The people were worshipping this dark angel, not knowing that it was a spirit of false religion.

Then, Father showed me what it meant: The crowds of people were not the throngs of some cult religion. Rather, they were major portions of the Church of Jesus Christ upon the earth. They were actively involved in their own methods of worship with little regard for the source of the light. They were going about their church business—some vigorously, some lethargically—but all with some level of commitment. Most of the worship and church business was being done out of guilt manipulation without a true and intimate relationship with the one honored.

These are the religious lost.

I was sent into the crowd to retrieve those who had died in the middle of worship of the dark angel. They were the ones who *knew* they were dead, not those who thought that their religious activities still held some life. This is a picture of the people and denominations that no longer make any hypocritical pretense of spirituality. They knew there was no life and they had become desperate for the return of the Holy Spirit breathing life into their dried bones. It is a mystery how I knew which ones to drag out of the crowd; it was simply evident that this identification was revealed by the Holy Spirit.

The act of speaking to the dead bodies brought them back to life. This illustrates the mission statement of Jesus when He read Isaiah 61 for those gathered in the synagogue:

"The Spirit of the Lord is upon me, because he hath anointed me to preach the gospel to the poor; he hath sent me to heal the brokenhearted, to preach deliverance to the captives, and recovering of sight to the blind, to set at liberty them that are bruised, to preach the acceptable year of the Lord."
Luke 4:18-19 KJV

As the people became whole enough to stand, they were immediately put to work dragging more dead out of the crowd and bringing others to life.

A spirit of false religion, that is, false spiritual authority, has deceived much of the church. This spirit appears as an angel of light, but its true motivation is binding the worshipers in darkness. I began to understand that this spirit of witchcraft was manifesting in the church as both control and religious spirits, using guilt manipulation and false spiritual authority. Well-meaning leaders had taken control of the sheep in an effort to keep them on the path of righteousness. However, such control and manipulation are what keeps Spectators impotent and distances them from the One with whom an intimate relationship should be developed. The man-made religious system designed to sustain the sheep is the very thing that has drained the power and intimacy out of the Body of Christ.

Our mission is made crystal clear in my vision: to reach into the organized religious system and bring out those who are desperate to know the life-giving breath of the Living God in spite of the bondage of their doctrine and in spite of their theological training. The harvesters miraculously find those who are dead and desperate, raise them from the dead, and the Lord of the Harvest sends them into the harvest fields to bring the true light of salvation and wholeness to the multitudes who will otherwise die in their deceptive religious stupor.

This vision is the initial impetus for despising what the organized church has perpetrated upon the people who call upon the Name of the Lord. Since that initial vision, the work has continued, and there are now many who have made the transition from deadness to life. What must be understood is that this kind of work cannot be done within the structure of the institutional church.

Hence, the glorious dynamic of basic church!

The only reason to go back into the traditional church is to find the dead and drag them out. The comfortable, seemingly safe pews of the structured church are seductive. It is much easier to sit and do nothing in the name of religious pride than it is to be trained to minister in your home and workplace. The simplicity of basic church combined with an active deliverance and wholeness ministry is the only way to real freedom. Drag them out, call them to life, deliver them, heal them in Jesus' name, then send them back into the throng.

THE PROMISED LAND

Needless to say, this vision and the prophetic word completely destroyed everything I thought I knew about the Kingdom and Father's view of church life. I found myself reeling from it. Everything came into question: my call, my vocation; my very life. During those early days I developed a friendship with John Cramer, a Nazarene pastor. As the Lord corralled me into this new paradigm of the church, John came alongside, helping me find perspective, challenging me, and caring for me. They were the most difficult days of my life. But John was there for me through the whole thing.

As I was making my exodus out of the institutional church, John wanted to come along, but in the end he stayed in the pastorate out of obedience to Father's call upon his life. In the years following my trauma, John and I became fast friends, which gave him the right to speak into my life. He still does so with astonishing precision.

John remained dubious about my journey since it was entirely opposed to his. One day while I was spouting off about the problems and challenges of this new paradigm, he quipped, "So, this house church thing is the Promised Land, is it?" My first reaction was to reach for my sword to defend my position with joy and vigor as I had so many times before. Instead, I contemplated his clever remark. Then it began to dawn on me, "Yes it is!" What follows is a paraphrase of the revelation that spilled out.

It took a series of plagues to uproot us from the relative comfort of our slavery. We went off into the desert with no concept of what lay ahead. We were pursued by the armies of the traditional church who were determined to bring us back to serve the institution's interests. Miracles occurred during our journey, but we were more concerned with what we *didn't* have. We wandered through the desert in fear for our spiritual lives. Then, when we got to the door of the Promised Land, we out-thought ourselves and rejected it. Soon, we were back running around the desert in confusion and poverty. We spent those years grumbling and complaining about lack, covetously eying the comfort of the padded pews of the very prison from which we escaped.

But something was happening out there: the old ways of thinking were dying off. After years of roaming, it was time to make our advance toward the Promised Land once again. Soon, we stood at the border, anticipating the gift Father had promised. But there was another surprise awaiting us: circumcision. After enduring the death of our theology and liturgy, He now demanded that something more personal be cut away. He excised our ego, our education, our experience, and our so-called wisdom.

He cut us to the quick.

After an extended time of recovery from the excruciating pain of His plan, we finally got to cross over into the Promised Land. Some of our friends had come as far as the river, but decided to stay on the other side, leaving us to fend for ourselves. More miracles occurred as our conquest began. Again we went brain-dead in our arrogance, determined to do it our own way.

On the heels of the miraculous victory at our Jericho, we endured the punishment for our Ai and finally resolved to follow His plan. Over the years, we warred with every conceivable giant—emotional, relational, mental, physical and spiritual—while moving from battle to battle. In the end, like the Israelites, we haven't been able to conquer the whole land. We remain oppressed on every border, waiting for the day when peace will come to this land.

"Yeah, John, I guess it is the Promised Land."

Many Escapees gravitate toward home groups. Others do absolutely nothing in terms of attending meetings. In any case, the Promised Land is not so much what we do or don't do, but *who we become* in this land flowing with milk and honey. Your Promised Land will reveal your personality and your spiritual giftings and will look quite different from ours. Your options include: simple church, open church, house church, and organic church; church in restaurants, in offices, in parks, in homes, by the pool, in the living room, and every sort of cyber church you can imagine. All in all, we like to call it Basic Church. The issue is no longer the form; it is now a maturing *relationship* with Father and with other Called Out Ones.

COACH'S TIP

Whether you are still in your Egypt, on the desert road, or in conquest of your Promised Land, Jesus promises:

"Take heart! I have overcome the world"
John 16:33.

Heal from your wounds, seek training in the new Promised Land paradigm, and go. . .

"drive out demons; . . . speak in new tongues; . . . place [your] *hands on sick people, and they will get well"*
Mark 16:17-18 (Brackets mine)

Chapter 3

The Great Escape

No One Gets Out Unscathed

The process of leaving a church is often excruciating. Church leaders respond predictably to your need and desire to follow what Father is instructing you to do. Initially they may seem to encourage you to actually attempt to move out and do something for the Kingdom. Pastors are forever hounding the Spectators to "go outside the four walls" or "move out in your gifting." However, embedded in the small print of these directives is the requirement for you do it *their* way, in *their* building, for the benefit of *their* empire. Our friend labels the dichotomy between the urging and the constraint: Mandatory but Prohibited.

Coach's Note:

Some of you may not connect with this section. Although many have benign experiences through the escaping process, the following is a compilation of what many others less privileged have faced.

When you balk at the constraints, the inevitable institutional head-game is initiated. First, you may be urged to remain in the fold for your spiritual safety. Leaders will be very concerned that you are heading into heresy, into rebellion, or that some evil influence has deceived you. This stage of the game is typified by the "We are concerned for your well-being" manipulation. Often, Escapees are delayed or even stymied by such tactics. It is entirely possible that the pastor may be functioning from a pure heart at this point since his paradigm does not allow for lay people to be out from under his "covering" or spiritual authority. He may be genuinely worried for your spiritual life. Even if that stance turns out to be untrue, let it be what it is. You will never be able to convince someone under the institutional mindset that the covering of which he speaks is anti-biblical and unnecessary.

If the first volley does not convince you that you must remain within the confines of the fold, the second trap is quickly set. This may be called the "We have been thinking that you would be perfect for this position" trap. Frequently, the position offered is beyond what you know you are capable of performing from the institutional mindset. Everyone understands that certain positions within the structure are held for those who have been deemed worthy and they are strictly off limits to the general church population. The job may be beyond your giftings or outside your experience but is nevertheless offered as an enticement to keep you in the church system. Many would-be Escapees fall prey to this diversion, so their escape is postponed or permanently foiled.

If you are not taken in by that move, the game may take a malicious turn. The final step in this hideous comic opera may be called the "You were never really loyal" accusation. This is quite clearly guilt manipulation of the gravest kind. The natural response to accusation propels you toward one of two ends: either defending your good name by proving that you are loyal by returning to your pew with your tail between your legs, or by jumping across the pastor's desk (literally or figuratively) to extend the right hand of fellowship to his nose.

We came alongside a couple of ladies who had an unusual version of this experience. They asked for their pastor's blessing to go and do what they felt Father was leading them to do, and he was magnanimous in his response. He blessed them in a public meeting and sent them out as if they were the church's missionaries. But when he realized that they were gathering Saints in their home without bringing them to his church on Sunday morning, he stood in front of the same people before whom he had blessed these ladies a few weeks before and actually withdrew his blessing. Astonishing!

When they heard about it, the ladies came to us for advice and comfort. We prayed for them, extended reassurance, spoke blessing over them, and encouraged them in their new adventure.

The reaction of church people—supposed friends and colleagues—is often the most surprising. Once you let it be known that you are gathering in a home to develop relationship with Father and with one another, you may be treated like a leper. You may lose many of the relationships you thought were strong. Resist the temptation to convince others to go with you. If they have the revelation for themselves, then receive them. If not, then consider yourself a pioneer: point your nose to the west and go. And don't judge those who stay behind.

GETTING OUT

The Sliders

As a result of many years of experience watching the absurdity of staying or going, I recommend door number three: *"Bless those who persecute you; bless and do not curse"* (Romans 12:14), and just slip right out with no fanfare.

We call it "the slide."

Since most people leaving the institution want to do so with the least amount of aggravation to both themselves and to the church, I recommend you quietly slide out and absorb whatever punishment leveled at you. Just tell them you are going away; ask for nothing; bless them; and slide out. Manipulation and accusations will follow you, but if you are tenacious and single-minded, you can simply disconnect from the gossip chain and not allow them to reach your ears. We have found that some of the healthiest Escapees are those who slide out rather than making a dramatic exit. We come alongside them to encourage and comfort them in the process while the system takes its shots.

Just go.

Tearing Away

Whereas sliding out is the best way, by far the greatest percentage of Escapees have terrible experiences escaping the institution. They are forced to tear themselves away from family and friends, traditions—both loved and despised—and from everything they have understood to be true Christianity. They feel as though parts of themselves have been torn out in the process.

Escaping church is often excruciating.

A DREAM

What follows is a dream that my wife Katie had in 1994. It helped us to crystallize our mission for the Escapees and not against the institution. At the time we were just attempting our initial escape from the pastorate and from the institution.

Tim and I were in a very large building with many floors and many rooms. We were looking for our "class," but each one was full. Finally, we found one with space available so Tim went in and settled right in with the other pastors. The rooms were full of sleeping pastors. Tim drifted off to sleep.

Someone told me that I had to be quiet and leave, so I went to the ladies' room and then just wandered the hallways, noticing the fine architecture and the quality of the furnishings.

Soon there were a few people walking through the halls. The sleeping people were starting to wake up and leave their rooms. I went to Tim's room where I found him already awake. He got up and dressed while many of the pastors in the room remained asleep. As we exited the room, there were many more people in the halls. People were waking up in many of the rooms.

We followed with the traffic flow not sure where we were headed. We came to a great staircase and made our way down. Toward the bottom of the staircase there was a woman, a bride, sprawled out in a lavish wedding gown that flowed down the stairs. She was thin and pale, but it was obvious that she was once very beautiful. She was so weak that she couldn't stand under the weight of the dress, which was once richly elaborate, but now dusty, dirty, and tattered. She kept struggling to stand, and occasionally would reach out or ask for assistance.

But the people just stepped around her.

They knew it was useless to stop and help, so they just passed her by. Shortly, what were hundreds in the halls now became thousands, all headed toward some unknown destination.

We reached several sets of doors of what seemed to be a great auditorium, perhaps seating over ten thousand. But we were stopped short and told that the auditorium was already filled to capacity. We were to take one of the buses to another facility. We boarded what appeared to be a sightseeing bus whose driver pointed out all the points of interest having to do with the place we had just left.

I started to recognize the place. We were dropped off at another church building and told that they had set up a large tent for us in the front yard of the church. It was to be just temporary until facilities were available. We were told that many churches now had tents set up in their yards as people came from all over the world.

In the front of the church building was a hole blown from the inside out as the result of an explosion. Amidst the debris, tents were set up to accommodate those who came out through the jagged holes. Soon we were caring for them in a triage set-up, tending to their wounds and preparing them to move out on their new adventure.

This is what the Lord showed Katie concerning her dream: This is a prophetic picture of what God is doing with His church. The sleeping pastors are those who are asleep in the religious systems of the world—safe and comfortable in a controlled and secure environment. But God is waking some from their deceptive slumber to a new calling, a new thing. Many others will miss the call and remain in the old traditions that they know and with which they are comfortable.

As these newly awakened Saints proceed down the stairs, they encounter a frightening picture: a once beautiful bride now weak and pale. She is unable to stand under the weight of the lavish religious tradition and ceremony she created for herself. That which she donned to make her beautiful for her groom has become burdensome and is now faded and worn out. The advancing throng moved around her, neither judging her nor stopping to help her, because they knew the task was impossible. Instead, they excitedly progressed to a new place to unite in worship and warfare for the Kingdom of God.

God is blowing out the walls of the building, drawing the Called Out Ones OUT where they can touch Him without the hindrances of the man-made religious structure of the corporate church. As with any new move of God upon the earth, this new move is forced outside the camp of organized religion into temporary places full of people of many denominations and creeds who are simply hungry to know Him. Because the walls are blown out, the people inside are not wounded by the blast. Rather, the explosion is from God to provide a means of escape. The people are joyfully worshipping and warring in the heavenly realms for the souls of lost men and women, both the heathen lost and the religious lost.

WHO IS OUT HERE WITH US?

The Called Out Ones are escaping. Whether through holes in the wall, open windows or right out the front door, they are leaving the institutional church in staggering numbers. It is not an organized, unified exodus; nevertheless, millions of true believers have given up on the traditional church and are simply leaving. Research reveals that somewhere between twenty and thirty million born again people have permanently left the traditional church structure.

So, cheer up! You are not alone.

Among this horde of Escapees are found people with five basic motivations. The Escapees whom you will receive into your homes and hearts in the years to come will be like one of these, so you must be prepared to meet their particular needs: to heal them, to equip them, and to send them out.

The Damaged

This is by far the largest group and it is made up of those suffering unhealed damage from spiritual abuse. The institution has become infamous for inflicting spiritual abuse on its members. These well-intended folks swallowed the propaganda of the institution only to be disappointed, discouraged, and denied at every turn. They have come to the conclusion that freedom is an arbitrary concept for others since it seems impossible for them to acquire.

Spiritual abuse is an enormous subject impossible to exhaust in these pages. However, the core of the issue lies in one word: control. The clergy are taught to control the sheep "for their own good." The clergy are controlled by the denomination "for their own good." The people of the denomination are controlled by church dogma "for their own good." And, finally, church dogma is controlled by a vast history of man's traditions designed to fill the void left by the absence of the active Presence of the Living God.

The traditions of men are the foundation of the modern church—both Catholic and Protestant—and we are held captive to the duplicitous devices of control and manipulation. In the process, the Saints are wrecked.

The Angry

The most vocal members of the exodus are the angry ones. They have given much—money, time, energy, and heart—only to discover that they remain second-class citizens within the clergy-dominated church structure. They are committed to submission to the hierarchy of the church system as a sign of "maturity." However, the Called-Out-One-spirit of kingship and priesthood (see Exodus 19:5-6) within us demands they grow into the natural and spiritual authority each one of them is promised.

The clergy system, by its very nature, is designed to restrict the laity. These constraints damage people as surely as chains injure the wrists and ankles of a prisoner. The constrained sheep become angry at the politics of the church, many begin to see conspiracy everywhere, and many others come to the place where they have an emotional blowout at an inopportune time. They may have undergone church discipline, whether warranted or not, resulting in deep resentment.

These kings and priests hate being told to stay in their place. It is absurd to be a king without being permitted to even rule one's own life. It is more absurd still to be a priest who is not a priest in action, since he/she has been duped into abdicating that role to a pastor. *"You have made them to be a kingdom and priests to serve our God, and they will reign on the earth"* (Revelation 5:10).

Many of those most angry are passive-aggressive in their response to the bondage. The core of their problem is unmet needs. Let's face it: the institutional church could be sued for false advertising. It offers freedom and liberty, healing and wholeness, only to exchange one set of chains for another. It asks, "Aren't you glad to be free?" while writing more and more church rules to restrict the saints. Instead of people getting angry and flying off the handle, the result is entrenched church politics and power plays. Few are angry outright. Oh no, that would be unspiritual! Instead, an inner fire quietly rages.

Generally, the only way these folks can be set free from their anger is through deliverance and deep inner healing. Once the deliverance session is over, Father will set out a plan to push their hot buttons until they deal with their issues. As they heal, they become worth their weight in spiritual gold. We have many friends who were once angry who now serve the Lord freely with joy and gladness.

The Rebellious

The most dangerous subgroup of Escapees is those who leave the institutional church just because they don't want anyone telling them what to do. These rebellious sheep are bound in their own authority issues and find it impossible to remain under the thumb of any leadership. Their church résumé typically reveals one exodus after another. They will attend a church for a while, serving in   a variety of positions, only to be quashed in their efforts to take control. Then, it's off they go to find a better church.

These folks have control issues, which they readily bring into the home group. They must be in charge or they won't play. They hate authority–perceived or actual–although they pretend to submit in order to gain favor. They are very dangerous to any group of Escapees.

It is possible to redeem them, though it will take persistence and a high tolerance for pain. The best way is to just be their friend. Spend time with them; give them your attention. This journey is perfect for them if they will submit to the revelation since, as we will explore in a later chapter, submission is mutual rather than positional.

However, we find that most of the rebellious ones are not happy unless they have a "following" of their own. The majority of those with whom we have had relationship have relapsed to their default paradigm, feeling "led" to create new empires for themselves. If this happens to someone you are befriending, it is recommended that you bless and let him or her go. Surprisingly, the constraints of the institution may be the only place where many of them can feel secure.

The Adventurous

The next Escapees are a delightful, albeit restless crowd. These folks are characterized by itchy feet. Anytime there is a new thing happening in the Body of Christ, the adventurous will show up, giddy with the prospect of something new. They love change and are enamored with the "new thing." It takes but a moment for them to become bored, so they accept anything new, no matter what it looks like.

The downside for the adventurous is that, in always seeking out the newest thing, they tend to get caught up in many of the marginally heretical teachings thriving in the Charismatic world. They are game for anything, so they are easily opened to corrupting influences. Many run to the new fad just for the sake of the adventure. On the bright side, these daring souls possess a pioneer spirit, craving to live in obedience to our "mobile" God. They generally love Him with all their being and are readily willing to sacrifice comfort for adventure. As you heal and equip them, you will not have to pacify their need for either security or stability because they require neither.

When adventurers come among you the best course of action is to try to get them to undergo training according to their giftings and personalities while keeping the door open for their certain and impending departure. That's right: they will leave you. That's what is supposed to happen. Take the time to provide healing, impart what you have, and release them to pioneer whatever unexplored territory Father indicates. The clergy hate their "unstable" ways because they are impossible to control. But they were born to be Escapees and pioneers. Hold them long enough to see their wounds healed and their giftings blossom, and then send them "where no man has gone before."

The Obedient

This is the easiest crowd to work with as they trek toward their Promised Land. They escaped the grip of the institution because they chose to be obedient to the Holy Spirit's directives. Recently, while discussing the contents of this book with a senior clergyman, he floored me with these words: "Anyone who has an ear to what the Lord is doing knows that this is precisely it."

The issue is clear: What will it take to get someone to obey? Will emotional and spiritual damage be enough? Or must indignation so consume us that we break through the walls and climb over the people of the church to get out? Should we nurture our base rebellious nature until it propels us out? It took ten plagues to get the children of Israel out of Egypt. Certainly the plagues were designed to convince the Pharaoh to let them go, but it was also to convince His people that He was orchestrating it.

36

Obedience should be enough.

Up and Down Staircase

Escapees are intrigued by the notion that "there must be more." We have found that the journey of recovering clergy is quite different from that of lay people. Those who were pastors simply jump off the precipice of clergydom, while lay people who have heard the same communiqué from the Holy Spirit must begin a climb out of laity's pit of obscurity. The clergy have attained what is purported to be the pinnacle of Christendom: the pastorate. They conquer their mountain and learn to rest on his lofty heights under the delusion that they are the only servants of the Most High. In actuality, it is in direct opposition to the idea of servanthood. What servant is so honored by his masters? What servant is at the head of the line? What servant is expected to teach his masters? What master obeys the teachings of his servant?

When the Escape revelation comes to a pastor's ears, the journey to the Promised Land is *downward*: losing position and privilege; losing honor; being humbled. I sat in the living room of one recovering pastor discussing his spiritual journey since escaping the pastorate. All at once, he turned to me and lamented, "Yeah, but I used to *be somebody*." People came to him for advice. He was honored for his preaching and administrative skills. Now he was (his words) "just like everybody else."

Coming to the simple truth that the position of "pastor" is both anti-biblical and impossible is enough to debilitate the best of them. They were trained to be a controlling and manipulative parent who couldn't allow the children to grow up "for their own good." They must now relinquish that power and face the truth of their own complicity in the spiritual abuse the institution imposed upon the people.

The path of recovering clergy is very difficult. If you are

one, find another with whom to make the journey. Or if you know one, take him in and care for him on his descent toward his Promised Land.

Conversely, the path of the laity is *up*. They have been relegated to the pews of sheepdom with few of the perks enjoyed by their clergy counterparts. When they hear Father's voice calling them to escape, many do so with the anticipation of something better, something that may release them into their own calling. They crave purpose and meaning in their lives. They advance toward the perks of their Promised Land with joy, while the recovering pastors descend with dread. When the journey ends—whether up or down—they all find themselves in the center of what Father desires, which is, ironically, that they are "just like everyone else." Life in the Promised Land is characterized by the fact that each of us is Father's favorite, His chosen child.

Everything else is gravy.

COACH'S TIP

When we obey, we do so, many times, to our own detriment. But just remember, there were no Holiday Inns on the prairie when the pioneers headed west. With the comforts of the institution far behind us, we press on.

"Therefore, holy brothers, who share in the heavenly calling, fix your thoughts on Jesus, the apostle and high priest whom we confess"
Hebrews 3:1

Chapter 4

Deprogramming

Running Naked Into the Woods

Sitting with a group of people who had just broken the bonds of their local institutional church, I found myself in need of answers to their most basic questions. "What do we do now?" and "Don't we need a covering?" and "How can we *be* the church without a church building?" They were both determined and giddy: determined to never go back, and dizzy at their own audacity at having the gall to escape.

"It's like escaping from prison," I said, "and running naked into the woods. There is a great sense of freedom having made it through the tunnels to the outside world. There is dancing and euphoria. But when the excitement dies down, you tend to notice that you made it out without any clothes or supplies, and it dawns on you, 'Hey, it's cold out here.' Then, you begin to take inventory of the resources for your survival, and to your horror, you find that you aren't equipped, you don't have the means or the ability to stay alive in this new environment."

"So, what do we do now?" The question is now more urgent, a sense of dread dripping from their lips.

"First, you survive," I quipped, knowing full well the implications of my words.

"Then, you overcome!"

SURVIVAL TRAINING

Having spent the last umpteen years warming the cheap seats of the institutional church, watching Pastor Perfection do his thing from the elevated pulpit, the Spectator, suddenly thrust from his comfort zone into the wilderness, is often lost, confused, and fearful. It is said that the average church person has heard enough sermons in his lifetime to equal a seminary degree in theology. The paradox is evident: we're highly educated, yet we are not equipped to overcome the simplest obstacle on our own.

This paradox reminds me of a professor I had in college. He was brilliant; he had several doctoral degrees to his credit. His teaching method was to turn his back on the students and write on the board for the duration of the class time. One day I made it to class just a couple of minutes late. I knew that I must hurry to get seated, get the notebook open, and catch up to his writing. As I wrote, I became aware of stifled snickering from the students around me. I looked up to see the professor writing feverishly on the board. He was wearing canary-yellow pants. But through the brilliant color of the slacks, one could clearly distinguish bright red hearts on his underdrawers.

It was said of him, "He is so smart he doesn't know enough to come in out of the rain." Escapees are in the same predicament. We know lots of Biblical information and doctrinal qualifiers, but little of it is applicable to our "real" lives.

Every new group of Escapees that invites us to come suffers from the same malady. They are well fed, yet ill prepared for the journey ahead. Spectators have long been relegated to watching ministry happen. They do not have the skills to get out of the pew and get into the fray. They remind me of Morgan Freeman's

40

character in the movie *The Shawshank Redemption*. When asked about his impending parole, he confesses the impossibility of living in the outside world:

He says, "I've been here most of my life. I'm an institutional man, now."

He had been stripped of the ability to make even simple decisions for himself. When he is finally released, he goes to work bagging groceries at the local supermarket. He asks the manager if he can go to the bathroom, to which the manager sarcastically replies that it is unnecessary to ask every time he needs to use the restroom.

He is so institutionalized that he just doesn't know how to live on his own.

Sadly, most Escapees are just like this character. We have been spoon-fed the Word with no requirement to feed ourselves. We have been given only the most rudimentary responsibilities within the institution garnering no skills to live on our own. I don't know how many times Escapees have wondered, "How will we get fed?" Here's a tip: feed yourself! I know the institution provided food at the same time each week upon which you subsisted. Now, however, the meals aren't prepared for you and slopped on your tray as you pass down the ecclesiastical chow line each Sunday. Instead, you must develop the skills to decide what you want to eat every day and then discover the joy of preparing and sharing the meal with your family.

This is the very point that attracts so many men who would never participate in the institution to escape. Men instinctively provide for their families. While men within the traditional church system are frequently emasculated, Escapee men are released to fulfill their hunter/gatherer destiny on behalf of their families. Asking a man to sit still while another person hunts and gathers the milk and meat of the Word of God for his family strips him of his authority and responsibility. On the road to his Promised Land, he will find the giftings necessary to find purpose. Then, he can truly stand as a "man of God," a term formerly reserved for that select few.

Since you have no hunter/gatherer training, at least early on, you may feel like you are starving. You have run naked into the woods without a pot to cook in or a plate to eat upon. Relax! Spectators are generally spiritually obese from eating spiritual food for years without exercising it off. Use this time to get into shape. Your stored fat will carry you until you learn to feed yourself.

DEINSTITUTIONALIZATION

Your recovery from institutionalism will take time. Give yourself permission to heal from your wounds caused by the chains. Take time to heal well. It is much the same as what one experiences grieving the loss of a loved one. The grieving process will take a similar route that Dr. Elizabeth Kubler-Ross describes as denial, anger, bargaining, depression, and acceptance, the acronym for which is: D.A.B.D.A..

D Usually, the first stage in the grieving process is **Denial**. This may take place without the knowledge or consent of the Escapee while still in the traditional church structure. There may be uneasiness as the realization of what is missing in the institution grows over time, or an inner voice that prepares one for the impending escape. During this step you may have found yourself digging in your heels and forcing yourself to find the good in the institution. Others report a growing unexplained irritation. In any case, we all undergo a denial of the true issues facing the church and ramp up our efforts to fix what's wrong or create a fresh approach to the same old issue.

Some of our Escapee friends have determined that they stayed in the church too long, much to their own detriment. They were committed to make something happen in the church—a reformation or a renewal—while their personal spiritual walk continued to decay. They tried with all their might to keep the institution alive all the while harboring an inner sense that it wouldn't work.

Almost everyone is praying for revival and renewal, but history shows us that every time Father moves upon the earth, the movement happens outside the established church. Even revivals like Azuza Street began in a small prayer meeting in a house. Apparently, Father will not break into the structure we have built in His name; He always goes outside the parameters of organized religion to show His power. However, the same scenario always follows Father's move: the movement is organized, synthesized, and sterilized and brought back into church structures. Soon, Father is obliged to go back outside the camp and reveal His presence once again.

It would astonish you to know how many traditional church pastors have confided to me, "You know what? Church doesn't work!" What intrigues me is that they continue to do the same thing over and over while expecting different results. Einstein said, "That's the definition of insanity." We continually retry the same programs or revamp the church system, only to be met with only inevitable limited success.

Denial is our friend.

A Stage two of the grieving process is **Anger**. This is the moment when the lie becomes clear and a wound is inflicted. We've been lied to: the clergy said the institution is God's plan for the Called Out Ones.

They lied. And now we're angry.

They said, "This is all there is," but we discovered there is a whole new reality out there. We've been held captive to another's vision, when we could have received vision of our own. We could have been a contender! Instead, we are barren, serving as a warm body to fill the pews and coffers of another's empire.

The anger grows as the revelation unfolds. We discover that the institution exists only to perpetuate itself while we are just a grain of sand on its vast sandy beach. It doesn't really matter if we are there or not; the institution will continue on unimpeded.

We find out how much we really lack. We lack spiritual authority. The pastor is serving as the "spiritual covering" over our family, a pseudo-Old Testament priest positioned between us and Father. We have abdicated the spiritual authority over our children to Sunday School teachers and youth workers. We have abdicated the responsibility for our spiritual growth to the pastor. We now discover to our horror that we are full-grown adults still crammed into the incubator of the traditional church structure.

The Called Out Ones are scrambling to know why we are here. What is our purpose? I have been appalled at the response to Rick Warren's **Purpose Driven Life**, not because of its message, but because it is a basic right of the children of the Living God to know their purpose and to live it out. The book's success only reflects the utter failure of the institution. Tens of millions of us had to buy a book to find out this rudimentary truth: we are important to Father and to His plan for the planet. We have a purpose.

A spiritual toddler should know that!

Over many years books have been offered to help people discover their spiritual gifts. But what good is it when we are not allowed to *function* in those gifts, unless they fit within the constraints of a pastor's vision? Knowledge of our giftings without the opportunity to exercise them only produces frustration.

Lots of Escapees are angry about discovering that all this time they have been serving a man instead of serving Father. Since the institution is designed around the position of pastor—

an extrabiblical invention of man—everything done is about him. We have expended energy to build *his* empire and have paid for *his* buildings and *his* vision.

When you are in this part of the cycle of grieving, you must resist the temptation to give someone a piece of your mind. We have found that many of the books over the past decade or so on the subject of house church have been written while the author is in the anger stage. It is only natural to want to vent when we are irate, but it has only served to alienate our brothers still captive within the institution.

"In your anger do not sin" (Ephesians 4:26), is the best advice for this time of anger. It is not a sin to be angry, but it *is* a sin to attack others simply to punish them for your hurt. So be angry, but do it well. Express it to Father and let the Holy Spirit soothe your pain. The most important thing is to encourage gatherings of Called Out Ones to not waste time sitting around venting their anger toward the institution.

As we connected with Escapees, we discovered that anger is usually their first expression. We offer our ears to let them vent without joining them in their rage. Our help is given in the form of coming along side in their hurt and listening. We offer no pat solutions for their heartburn, only a loving arm to lean upon. Remaining in the anger for too long is counterproductive. Once Escapees have vomited their pain for a while, we wipe their brow and press them toward healing. Encourage one another to *"bless those who persecute you; bless and do not curse"* (Romans 12:14). We recommend *The 2 Minute Miracle* by M. Lynn Reddick as a blessing guide.

B Following the anger stage, we naturally move into **Bargaining**. After enduring the pain of the escape, people may be tempted to backtrack and fantasize: "Maybe church *does* work." It is the same seduction of perceived comfort the Israelites expressed when they craved the leeks and garlic of Egypt. Life as an escapee is exhausting. We are constantly moving; we have to feed ourselves; no one tells us which way to go; it seems that we are living out the Apostle Paul's job description:

> *"For it seems to me that God has put us apostles on display at the end of the procession, like men condemned to die in the arena. We have been made a spectacle to the whole universe, to angels as well as to men. We are fools for Christ, but you are so wise in Christ! We are weak, but you are strong! You are honored, we are dishonored! To this very hour we go hungry and thirsty, we are in rags, we are brutally treated, we are homeless. We work hard with our own hands. When we are cursed, we bless; when we are persecuted, we endure it; when we are slandered, we answer kindly. Up to this moment we have become the scum of the earth, the refuse of the world."*
> 1 Corinthians 4:9-13

During this step, some of our brethren return to the "Egypt" of the institution. We seldom discourage this action since we make it a habit not to tell anyone what to do. Escapees are learning to exercise spiritual authority over themselves for the first time and it is ridiculous to usurp it as the system does, even if we think what they are doing is wrong. Some will go back to church to stay, living in a sort of permanent denial of their own making. We have many close friends who have decided to return to "Egypt." The development of their fledgling spiritual gifts is often arrested as they resign themselves to the barrenness of life within the institution. Denial reemerges in the form of "We need the worship" or "This time we will do it right" or "We're doing it for our children."

Others try to go back and are met with a rude awakening, only to run to once again from the bondage. They sample the leeks and taste the garlic momentarily only to become disgusted with the bitter compromise.

I am one of these.

After escaping church and the pastorate in 1994, I continued my recovery for a few years, meeting in homes and experiencing the power of God as never before. We broke up a traditional church into small groups meeting in homes. We trained the leaders as best we could, and then released them to do the works of service to which Father had called them. It was a smash hit for a while, but soon some of the Called Out Ones began craving the leeks and garlic of Egypt. They grumbled and complained and then went back to the church.

Most of us stayed on the journey toward the Promised Land. However, over time, the enticement of the leeks overcame most of the leadership team and, late in 1997, I agreed to start another traditional church. Our particular leeks and garlic consisted of children's ministry, teen ministry, and corporate worship. At first, the Sunday morning meetings were powerful. The momentary freedom we had experienced outside the institution carried over into the Sunday morning meetings and it was wonderful. But organization soon followed, crushing the life out of us. It took me a few years to escape again. I ensured that the people who stayed behind were pastored as they desired, and this time my family and I left the institution alone.

We have never looked back.

The bargaining stage is inevitable. Be prepared for it and move through it. If you do go back to your Egypt, good for you! If you resist it, press into the Holy Spirit and He will carry you through to your Promised Land.

D The next step in the grieving process represents what is for most the low point. Perhaps **Depression** is best revealed in the question: "Is this all there is?" Manna was a miracle as the Israelites trekked through the desert, but the same thing every day gets old.

Really old.

It is like the vacation from hell: driving across the country with the kids and dog in the station wagon day after day after day. Being constantly on the move away from Egypt toward the Promised Land is exhausting. No matter what you do, you can't rush the process. You must plod across the dusty miles until you reach the goal. Of course, if you do it the way I did the first time, with a whole group of people, you will hear the inevitable whine from the back seat: "Are we there yet?"

Depression is a sense of inevitability weighing heavily upon your shoulders. Moving out into a pioneering effort is initially exciting, but the difficulties of the trip soon strip away all idealism. Then reality rushes in. We discover the lack of resources and support networks; we don't know where we are or what we are doing. Many Escapees succumb to depression and just sit down on the trail.

It's okay. Sit down and rest. Ask Father for a visitation of His presence. Depression will allow you to rest and find refreshment for the next leg of the journey. Soon you will hear Father's voice coming from somewhere ahead, "Saddle up, son. We're moving out."

Depression left unchecked is a severe problem. Nonetheless, it is a natural part of life on this planet. I suffered from its effects for many years. One time I asked the Lord why He didn't just take it away. His answer made perfect sense: "I use your depression as a time to speak to you. When you are busy and productive, I can't seem to get a word in edgewise. When you are depressed, you sit down long enough to hear my voice."

Am I advocating depression as a lifestyle? Of course not. But when it comes, stop focusing upon it and turn your eyes to the hills, because it's from there that your help comes (see Psalm 121).

Then, when Father urges you, get up and follow Him. There's fun ahead.

A Finally, we come to **Acceptance**. The good news is that healing is out there ahead of you; the bad news is that it may be years away. I figure it took me about eight years to fully recover from my institutional paradigm. Of course, I was a clergy person perpetuating the lie within the institution, so I was a hard case. Many of our friends report similar timeframes, but you might do it quicker.

Remember this about the grieving process: you don't take a series of well-ordered steps and then disembark into the Visitor's Center of the Promised Land. What is more likely is that you will cycle through all five stages a number of times, not necessarily in the same order, as you move through deeper levels of healing. Relax! If you mess it up the first couple of times, you're likely to get another chance to do it right.

This raises a question: "Can this be done?" My advice is simple: decide that this is an adventure. People spend millions of dollars every year to experience adventures. Some put their lives on the line to hunt lions or to climb a mountain, while others go to a theme park and let someone heave them over the top of a roller coaster while they scream their lungs out. We all crave adventure. Maybe your desire for adventure is less dramatic, perhaps something like a trip to the country on the weekend. Whatever your brand of adventure, be sure Father will stretch your definition to more closely align with His. This is the grand adventure of all time. Your eternal life is at stake, along with the lives of those you will be privileged to touch along the journey.

It is the ultimate adventure.

TAKE TIME TO HEAL

As you cycle through the stages of grief, the result is the deinstitutionalization of your entire being. Your mind needs to be freed from its chains. You will discover that you are not a "sinner saved by grace" but a real live Saint. The New Testament never calls us sinners; we are called "saints" more than two hundred times. There is real freedom in knowing our place in the Kingdom of God.

Your emotions need healing. Your body needs healing. Your relationships need healing. Your finances need help. The process of deinstitutionalization will affect every possible aspect of your life as unbiblical and anti-biblical religiosity is replaced by the authentic freedom found in the Kingdom of Light.

COACH'S TIP

Be quick to recognize the hold the institution still has upon your soulish areas–your mind, your will, and your emotions–and focus your attention to eliminate that old way of thinking. Chase every bit of institutional thinking from your being! It may take months, perhaps years, but the end result is real liberty.

"Live as free men, but do not use your freedom as a cover-up for evil; live as servants of God"
1 Peter 2:16.

Chapter 5

EXPLORING THE PROMISED LAND

STARTING AT THE BEGINNING

Now that you have a handle on what your personal process will be over the next few years, it's time to spy out this new land. You are unaccustomed to this new environment, so look out! There are giants in the land! But you are up to the task, since "[you] *can do everything through him who gives* [you] *strength*" (Philippians 4:13, brackets mine).

THE MAJOR LEAGUES

While you are more mature in Christ than you have been allowed to know, you are still a Promised Land rookie. Think of your situation like that of a professional baseball player who finally makes it to the Major Leagues. He has played baseball ball his whole life—T-Ball, Little League, Babe Ruth, American Legion, Junior Varsity, Varsity, college, Rookie ball, Single, Double, and Triple A Minor League ball—but when he comes up to the Majors for the first time, he is considered a rookie. Does it mean he doesn't know anything about the game? Does it demean anything he has learned at the lower levels? Of course not. But it is a considerably different environment in the Big Leagues, and he is the new kid on the field.

In the same way, you have known the church game for years, maybe decades. You have come through everything from the Cradle Roll to the Deacon Board over the years.

You know the game.

And yet, this is entirely different out here. Remember that everything you have learned in Egypt is now suspect. The safest way to proceed is to assume that what you know probably is corrupted by the institutional paradigm, so take the time to start at the beginning.

The beginning is **family**.

TO DO OR NOT TO DO

Once we abdicate the spiritual authority of our families to the clergy, pastors and priests make policy decisions for our homes and dictate how we are to live. We relinquish spiritual responsibility for our children to well-meaning but spiritually unhealthy Sunday School teachers and youth leaders, expecting them to shoulder the burden of training our children in the ways of the Lord.

Here's a simple answer to the question, "Where do we begin?" Gather with your family. Start with what you already have. Maybe that means parents with children who still live at home. If you are single, divorced, or "empty-nesters," get together with others who share your situation, or blend singles and couples, and families with children together.

Such a prospect may be scary, for many Escapees believe they don't truly know Father's ways, nor do they feel equipped to mentor others in the intricacies of Biblical faith. Sadly, despite years of hearing sermons and various teachings, many folks have retained little that might prove practical in facing the challenges of real life.

The Hebrew concept of teaching is expressed in this wonderful piece of Scripture:

> *These commandments that I give you today are to be*
> *upon your hearts. Impress them on your children. Talk*
> *about them when you sit at home and when you walk*
> *along the road, when you lie down and when you get*
> *up. Tie them as symbols on your hands and bind them*
> *on your foreheads. Write them on the doorframes of*
> *your houses and on your gates."*
> Deuteronomy 6:7-9

It's not about meetings. If you have a meeting, it will quickly degrade to your default training. And what is that training? Institutionalism. It's all Escapees know. So when you run out of creative ideas for your meetings, you will slip backward and once again walk like an Egyptian.

Don't do meetings. Don't do church.

When Katie is asked where and when we go to church she is fond of remarking, "I've been to church seventeen times this week." It always startles the person who asked since we've been trained that church is an *event* rather than a *state of existence*. The reverse is the real truth.

A friend of ours pastored for years before the Lord called him out of the traditional church setting into the home. He didn't know what to do, so he built himself a portable, folding pulpit and lined up some of those nasty metal folding chairs in rows … in his living room!

He reverted to the only thing he knew: church.

FAMILY, CLAN, TRIBE, AND NATION

Though it is taken from an unfortunate story, the following Scripture elucidates the four stages of relationship within the people of God, the children of Israel, as well as the Called Out Ones today:

> *Early the next morning Joshua had **Israel** come forward by **tribes**, and Judah was taken. The **clans** of Judah came forward, and he took the Zerahites. He had the clan of the Zerahites come forward by **families**, and Zimri was taken. Joshua had his family come forward man by man, and Achan son of Carmi, the son of Zimri, the son of Zerah, of the tribe of Judah, was taken.*
> Joshua 7:16 (Bold mine)

The Family

Not other people's family, but *your* family. These people are your blood kin. If you do not have any family, skim this part. We will get to your mission in a moment.

One of the most common reasons given for leaving a church is, "We weren't being fed." Here's wisdom: feed yourself!

The issue is very clear: we church people don't know how to feed ourselves. Moreover, we have been taught to believe that it is anti-biblical, and maybe even sinful to take care of our own spiritual feeding. This is the watershed moment of this book: *Saints must learn to feed themselves.* It doesn't mean that we can't or won't be taught by others, but that *we*, not the clergy, are now solely responsible for our spiritual food and the spiritual food of our families.

Do you want to change your nation? Start by doing something about your marriage. Go to marriage seminars, read books, but most of all choose to love your spouse as Christ loved the Called Out Ones.

Want to change the educational system? Do something about your kids. Church kids are as rebellious and carnal as those in the secular culture. They are having sex at the same rates as heathen kids; they are doing drugs and getting drunk just like their heathen counterparts. The only antidote for this plague is mothers and fathers wrenching the reins of their kids' lives from the institutional professions—whether church or public school—and feeding them from the riches of the Kingdom of God.

So how is this part of the elephant to be devoured? Stop ministering to other people and focus your attention upon your own kids. Teach them, train them, and put them to work in the Kingdom of God.

Family church is the first step to deinstitutionalizing the Called Out Ones.

The Clan

The "clan" is the extension of your blood kin to those around you. Friends and neighbors who are part of your sphere of influence will comprise your clan. Bring them into you home frequently and develop fellowship around the table, the pool, or just sitting in the back yard fighting off the mosquitoes. But let them know *you* and get to know *them*.

The key to this relationship building is learning to create a sense of belonging. What does that look like? We call it "refrigerator rights." If you have "refrigerator rights" in someone's home, you have moved past being an acquaintance, past being a friend, until you are one with each other, sharing all good things.

As this deep fellowship is developed, begin approaching Father together–as an extended family. Remember, the default position for everything among the Called Out Ones is the family, as opposed to structured meetings. Since we are recovering institutional thinkers—trained to just do religious things with strangers—this step may be daunting. Because of the Blood of the Lamb running through your veins—and through their veins—you are genuine blood kin as much or more than those of your human family.

Our holiday feasts and frequent clan gatherings include a whole variety of people. We rarely schedule stuff, since that seems too institutional. Instead, we just put out the word and the clan comes a-runnin'. Our favorite thing is to set the back yard on fire (otherwise known as a bonfire) and sit around talking about life, about family, about problems and victories, and of course, about Father. In this casual context, some really cool stuff happens. One word of caution: though "clan" is the biblical word for such a gathering, we just call the clan gatherings "family dinner" since "clan meeting" means something unfortunate, especially in the South.

What if you were born into my family instead of yours? What would change in your life? You would look like a different person, more like my parents than yours. You would think like my father and mother, and act more like my mother and father. Your life would be entirely transformed from who you are now to look like your new family.

Isn't that the definition of coming into the "family of God?" We were born into sin; once, we looked, thought, and acted like our birth family. But since coming into this *new* family—being *"born again"* (see John 3:3)—we are being *"transformed by the renewing of our minds,"* (see Romans 12:1-3) no longer conforming to the pattern of our first birth family.

The Tribe

The daily life of the Called Out Ones is consumed with the family and the clan. These relationships are cultivated constantly with care. From time to time, it seems fun to invite a larger group together to celebrate one of the Old Testament feasts or to hold some regional conference or seminar for the good of everyone within that sphere of influence. This may be related to the Saints in Ephesus or at Galatia to whom some of Paul's letters were written. There wasn't just one group within each of those cities; the letters were written to a greater gathering of the Saints of the city who would come together on occasion. The "Galatian" believers of that region were grouped together as a whole for certain specific instances though they gathered as family and clan most of the time. These invitees aren't people with whom we have daily interaction. They are friends from our city or region who are surely part of us, and we them, from whom we may glean some spiritual truth or develop some new family or clan relationship.

This is the gathering of the tribe.

These gatherings are only occasional, since the logistics of pulling such a large group together at one time in one place are extensive. However, many cities currently hold such meetings to reinforce the tribe relationship that extends past the parameters of the family and the clan.

What passes for the tribe is the institutional church. But the tribe is not intended to gather weekly or more often. Intimacy is lost in these groups and relationship can be only cursory. Gathering the tribe too often is counterproductive to spiritual health since responsibility must be abdicated to some leader and participation is necessarily limited by the large group. If you give yourself to weekly gatherings of the tribe the cherished oneness of the family and clan gatherings vanishes.

Consider this: the New Testament definition of what we call Christianity is found in a confrontation between Jesus and some Pharisees. They challenged Him:

"Teacher, which is the greatest commandment in the Law?" Jesus replied: "'Love the Lord your God with all your heart and with all your soul and with all your mind.' This is the first and greatest commandment. And the second is like it: 'Love your neighbor as yourself.' All the Law and the Prophets hang on these two commandments."
Matthew 22:36-40

57

What is this Kingdom walk all about? Relationship with Father and relationship with one another. Most churches focus upon the first part in a sterile context they often only nod at the second. Developing a relationship with someone cannot be accomplished while looking at the back of their head for an hour or two once a week. It must be daily interaction in real life situations.

We will expand this thought a few chapters from now.

The Nation

We hold a couple of celebrations a year, one during the season of Passover and Pentecost and another during the Feast of Tabernacles. These feasts were given to the Jews and have been inherited by the Saints in the New Testament age. We recommend that the central focus of such gatherings be Father, Jesus, the Holy Spirit, and celebration. Make it a big party. Teach some stuff if you must, but celebrate the presence of the Lord and celebrate one another.

Because we recovering church-a-holics will easily succumb to the corporate jazz of bigger gatherings, it is recommended that these times of convocation be limited to a few times every year. The Children of Israel lived in daily relationship with their family and clan, but from time to time, they made pilgrimages to the larger gatherings of the tribe, as well as the nation as a whole.

The family, clan, tribe, and nation should know how to interact and should be aware of their relationship with one another, while living routinely in the arms of family and clan. This model provides protection, strength, and relationship from which new families, and new clans will grow. We believe this model—designed by Father and utilized among His children in the Old Testament—is the divine pattern for life as His children for all time.

COACH'S TIP

Nurture family and clan relationships.
Find helpful seminars and conferences to stretch
your ways of thinking among the tribe.
Celebrate the feasts with joy with the whole nation of Saints.
Feed yourself; feed your family; eat well a
nd may your bones be fat!

*"Let's see how inventive we can be in encouraging love
and helping out, not avoiding worshipping together as
some do but spurring each other on, especially as we
see the big Day approaching."*
Hebrews 10:21-25 The Message

Chapter 6

THE HOW-TO'S OF FAMILY LIFE

THE FAMILY GATHERING

The imperative for healthy family life is reproduction and the raising of children. We all come from families with one level of dysfunction or another. As we develop our understanding of the spiritual family and clan, those dysfunctions provide us with a wonderful template of what NOT to do as we birth and raise babies in Christ.

As we move through the following sections, there are dual themes. The first is obvious: *"Train up a child in the way he should go: and when he is old, he will not depart from it"* (Proverbs 22:6). The second theme concerns the people with whom you will gather—at home, at school, at the office, or in the back yard. As you equip your own children, create relationships with other Called Out Ones and serve one another with these same principles. Let those young in the Lord practice their gifts. Model for them and mentor them, then get out of the way and let them do it.

Notice the phrase "one another" in the paragraph above. Instead of one person functioning as the all-knowing-all-seeing-eye resembling the position of pastor, discover the joy of learning from one another. As each matures in spiritual gifts, he/she must be poured into the others to create a rich fellowship. When you have friends over to your house it is a perfect time to practice what is the only instruction in the New Testament concerning what to do when we get together. The important point here is that each person offers something to the group. As the Holy Spirit moves through the Saints, notice that no one has exclusive rights to the floor. Everyone is encouraged to participate. This is how "basic church" functions:

> *When you come together, everyone has a hymn, or a word of instruction, a revelation, a tongue or an interpretation. All of these must be done for the strengthening of the [Called Out Ones]. If anyone speaks in a tongue, two—or at the most three— should speak, one at a time, and someone must interpret. If there is no interpreter, the speaker should keep quiet in the church and speak to himself and God. Two or three prophets should speak, and the others should weigh carefully what is said. And if a revelation comes to someone who is sitting down, the first speaker should stop. For you can all prophesy in turn so that everyone may be instructed and encouraged. The spirits of prophets are subject to the control of prophets. For God is not a God of disorder but of peace ... Therefore, my brothers, be eager to prophesy, and do not forbid speaking in tongues. But everything should be done in a fitting and orderly way.*
> 1 Corinthians 14:26-40
> (Brackets mine: replacing "church" with its definition.)

BE CALLED OUT ONES

> *These commandments that I give you today are to be*

*upon your hearts. Impress them on your children. Talk
about them when you sit at home and when you walk
along the road, when you lie down and when you get
up. Tie them as symbols on your hands and bind them
on your foreheads. Write them on the doorframes of
your houses and on your gates."*
Deuteronomy 6:7-9

Instead of doing church, be Called Out Ones. It may seem like an abstract idea to a Spectator such as yourself, but it is the centerpiece of life in the Promised Land. Break down the verses from Deuteronomy above to glean the concept.

"Impress them on your children." You, Mom and/or Dad, not someone else. Take responsibility for them. The pastor and the Sunday School teachers mean well, but you must step into that breach. The responsibility for what they know and who they become is yours alone.

Ever wonder why it has become an inevitable truth in modern society that teenagers must rebel? It's because we have allowed others to shape their morals and beliefs from birth. If a daycare worker raises your children eight or ten hours a day and the kids sleep ten to twelve hours, how much of *you* is really integrated into their heart and mind? I have had lots of parents sitting in my office weeping because they can't figure out where their kids learned to act the way they do.

News flash!

If, as we are told by psychologists, the personality of the child is set by about age five and she has spent most of her time in daycare, then it only makes sense that the daycare worker's character is what you are reaping when she turns fifteen and loses her mind. When my son Lucas was sixteen, he came to me one day and said, "Dad, I was wondering if it would be all right if I rebelled a little?" I looked at him and said, "Listen, I don't think you really have the concept of rebellion down very well.

But what do you have in mind?" Soon, his hair was freakishly long, he got a tattoo, and he got earrings in both ears.

Big deal.

Did Lucas ever do anything stupid growing up? Sure. But he was always redeemable. His DNA is full of Jesus, whether he likes it or not. Today, he walks with Father with four kids of his own. He still has the tattoo and the holes in his earlobes, but his rebellion was not permanent. We talk about the things of life just as we did when he was young. His mom and I were the ones who shaped his personality in those formative years. We did not let the culture steal him from us. We taught him to love Jesus and to live as a Saint.

But, But, But

If you are a single parent and daycare is your only option, then try to find someone who reflects your moral fiber. If you, as a Called Out One, can take in children of other Saints who must leave their children to work, then do it immediately. We must care for the widows and the fatherless. It is our mandate. This is part of our Promised Land responsibility.

On the other hand, if you are a husband and wife team raising children and you leave your children at daycare, you are risking your kids' future for a bigger house and a nicer car. If it takes both your incomes to make ends meet, get a smaller house, buy an older car, or sell the television. Whatever you do, one of you should be home with the child at least for the first five years. It is much better to downgrade your lifestyle for a while than to reap rebellion later on. Stop letting the "must have it now" culture dictate your child's future. Wrest authority over your family from the grip of humanism and consumerism.

You probably think I'm a throwback to the days of Father Knows Best, but the future of the Called Out Ones depends upon this alteration. Sure, it seems very counter-culture to shun "stuff" for the sake of our families. But it's time to stop reaping someone else's traits from ten years ago that now may destroy your relationship with your children for a lifetime.

Just a note here: If Mom can make more than the Dad in the marketplace, then it is perfectly proper for Dad to be Mr. Mom. I did it myself for a while when our kids were small. I was attending college and Katie ran her own business. I cooked, cleaned, and changed messy diapers. The only thing I couldn't master was laundry—all those colors and whites, and hot and cold, and detergent and fabric softener … I still don't get it.

TALK

"Talk about them when you sit at home, and when you walk along the road, when you lie down and when you get up." Books, videos, and storytelling, it's a three-point plan. Read to your kids. Get them videos that teach Biblical principles. Tell bedtime stories, suppertime stories, and stories in the car or on the couch. Make the precepts of the Word of God a constant source of discussion. If you are one of those who don't talk much—change.

Change right now.

We have chats with our grandchildren about the adventures of Bob and Larry (Veggietales). The kids can tell the stories because they have watched the videos a thousand times. We just make the stories relate to real life.

As the children get older, talk with them constantly. Take them to the store and talk about their life. Sit down to dinner and talk about life as a Called Out One. Eliminate all Christianese lingo and integrate the principles of the Word into real life until there is no separation between the sacred and the secular. This partition between "real life" and church life has been the downfall of many family units.

As I was growing up, we were required to have "devotions"

every day after supper. It consisted of my dad reading the Bible or some devotional material as we sat at the table yearning to get back outside to play ball or go fishing, anything fun. It wasn't wrong; it was just what Christians were told to do.

When I got married and had kids, I started to perform the same ritual, since that was my default understanding of how it was to be done. I discovered that I was just as bored with devotions as an adult as I was as a kid.

We never did it again.

Instead, we played ball or fished or did something fun, all the while integrating the precepts of Jesus. When my daughter Heather was at Oral Roberts University, she called one day and said something interesting. As she took her Bible classes she discovered, to her amazement, that she knew much more of the Word and its precepts than she realized. She had absorbed Father's heart and His Word without lecture-style teaching or formal devotions. It was a very real part of who she was, as opposed to information she retained only for an exam.

So, here is wisdom: talk ... and listen.

REAL LIFE

Why have meetings? *Everyone* is bored in meetings. A Saint's life must not be confined to meetings. Make life as a Called Out One fun and interesting. It can be done! If you make the Bible a daily part of life—as opposed to setting it apart only for special occasions—your kids will be full of its precepts when they are grown. Do not do a little institution in your house. The kids even hate church when it is done well, with the professional band and the slick orator doing all the talking. Make it about stuff that is really going on in their lives, while life is happening.

"Tie them as symbols on your hands and bind them on your foreheads. Write them on the doorframes of your houses and on your gates." These two sentences simply say, "Make the Word

appear everywhere." Our society makes available the innumerable modern language versions of the Bible. I recommend that you set the King James Version aside and integrate a version that can be quoted in everyday language without the hearer necessarily knowing that what you just said was Scripture. The Message Bible is a wonderful tool for such a goal. Why not absorb the Word for everyday use instead of acting all self-righteous about quoting chapter and verse.

When my kids were small, I set about changing from the King James—upon which I was raised—to the New International Version for just such a purpose. If it is true that *"... the word of God is living and active. Sharper than any double-edged sword, it penetrates even to dividing soul and spirit, joints and marrow; it judges the thoughts and attitudes of the heart"* (Hebrews 4:12), then it does not require chapter and verse, or to be read in your stained-glass voice to make it powerful. If you integrate it subtly into your daily language, it will still accomplish its work unimpeded by the resistance created when you come off sounding like a television evangelist.

REPROGRAMMING

Parents must be re-taught how to mentor their children. The gathering of the clan is not the place to teach the kids. However, it is the place to put what they have learned through your daily mentoring into practice.

Parents participating in home groups often complain about what to do with the children. This is hold-over institutional thinking. Christianity is for the children. Sending them to Children's Church so that they don't disrupt the sacred sermon is nothing less than an abomination.

Open participation means open participation.

Kids should take part in worship.

They are natural singers and dancers, and the living room is the best place to let them loose. Sing along with CD's or without any instruments, the effect will be the same. If you want to know what kind of worship makes Father happy, watch the kids, especially those under age five.

Kids should take part in ministry.

Your children don't have to undergo intense inner torment to discover what their gifts are. As you mentor them, they will demonstrate who they are in everyday situations. From a young age my youngest daughter, Amber, gravitated toward situations where healing was needed. Even when I was still pastoring in the traditional church I knew enough to bring her with me when praying for the sick. I showed her how to lay her hands on them and how to command healing in their bodies. Often people received healing through her hands.

Let them do it!

It's not about the prayer or the prophecy; it's about equipping the next generation to do the works of service. Show the kids how to do it and get out of the way. Use this same principle to train others with whom you meet.

During the renewal of the 1990's, the Lord moved powerfully through us as people couldn't stand up under the power of God and fell to the ground, sometimes paralyzed for long periods of time. Others were tickled in their beings so that hysterical laughter erupted from their bellies. In our meetings, peopled lined up for me to release the Presence of God upon them. Early in the renewal, I set about training ministry teams of lay people (since we were still in the institution) to pray over the people, and the pastoral staff served as coaches. Instead of the focus of the move being me, Father became the focus.

This renewal began just before we broke the church up into home groups. By the time the small groups were formed, the people were equipped to minister to each other without expecting the clergy hired-gun to run the show. The kids were trained to release His Presence as well. It was great fun.

So, what do we do with the kids? Let them participate in everything. Sure, it may seem like chaos at first, but be patient. Eventually, they will know how to minister as you guide them along the path.

GET TOGETHER

Modern life is increasingly about isolation. Soon, we will not have to leave the house for anything. You can order anything you need online and have it delivered to your door. Many business people are opting to work at home via the Internet and the phone instead of commuting to the office every day. We find our spouses online through find-a-mate services. Relationships are built not through face-to-face friendships, but through chat rooms.

This is a double-edged sword. On the one hand, it makes it possible to stay among the children and be a force in their daily lives. But it also isolates us from relational interaction with others.

Once you get settled into ministering to your own family, it is time to adopt others into your family unit. Adoption is a fundamental precept of Kingdom life. Adopt another family or single people to be part of your family. Get together and barbeque. Grab a cup of coffee and a doughnut. Go to the park. Hang out.

Gather your new blended family together and talk about Jesus. Make it simple. Make it real. Make it interesting. This is your clan. I don't think *". . . where two or three come together in my name, there am I with them"* (Matthew 18:19) is a metaphor. I think it is Jesus' plan for His kids to get together. When more than two or three get together, trouble seems to follow. We have been duped into thinking bigger is better. It's another lie! Less is more in the Kingdom of God.

If you are a single person with no blood family with which to mingle, you should be adopted into another family unit. The new family may consist of other singles or a combination of singles and married couples. In this new land, no one is left to fend for him or herself.

A Six-Point Plan

Called Out Ones love points and steps and keys, so here are six to make you happy. What follows are the keys to progressing into relationships with other Saints. They may seem profound, but I'm sure that, with some study, anyone can follow them.

1. Invite some friends to eat.
2. Get to know one another in your environment.
3. Go to their house and eat.
4. Get to know them in their environment.
5. Go out to eat
6. Only when you know their heartbeat, pray for one another, prophesy to each other, and otherwise enjoy 1 Corinthians 14:26:

"When you come together, everyone has a hymn,
or a word of instruction, a revelation, a tongue or
an interpretation. All of these must be done for the
strengthening of the [Called Out Ones]"
(Brackets mine: replacing the word "church"
with the definition.)

Doubtless you've discovered the key word among the six points: *eat*. The Greek word translated "fellowship" in the New Testament is *koinonia*. We got a wonderful picture of this word one Thanksgiving when we invited a Middle Eastern woman to share our table. She taught us the word picture for *koinonia* as we ate.

When a family sat down to eat in Bible times, typically one big bowl would be set in the middle of the table containing meat, vegetables and a broth. Each in attendance would be given a large piece of bread. They would dip the bread into the bowl and use it to grasp some meat or some vegetables while it got saturated in the broth. They would take the portion to their mouth and eat. Then, with the remainder of the bread, they would reach back in and get more until the bread was gone.

Double dipping! A social faux pas of the greatest magnitude, at least for Westerners!

But what really happens with the second dip? Your germs—you—are put into the bowl. When the person sitting next to you follows your lead and reaches in for his second dip, what does he get?

You.

By the simple act of eating together you become part of one another, not in some ethereal, philosophical sense, but in reality. You take the other person into you and he takes you into him. You are now forever linked together through this meal. This explains why it was so important in Eastern cultures to share a meal.

So when two or three of you get together, eat something, have a sandwich or a cup of coffee. You don't have to double-dip your Oreo cookie in other people's milk to experience *koinonia*, but seeing them talk with their mouth full of that black goo certainly breaks down inhibitions and allows you to get to know one another at a deeper level. Even business people know the benefit of doing business over a meal. It engenders fellowship.

As you get to know others, ask about their spiritual journey; tell yours. Share concerns; pray for one another. Allow prophecy to flow or tell them what you've been learning from the Holy Spirit.

This is real "church."

BIG MEETINGS

Wait until you can be trusted not to covet the leeks and garlic of the large group meeting before you allow yourself to get a bigger group together. Do it once in a while if you like, but don't allow one another to be seduced by its comforts.

Large groups are not evil; they're just less advantageous to our spiritual health. We still get together in a larger group sometimes to sing and dance before the Lord. I think that the days of large stadiums full of worshippers is not far off—as others have written—but those gatherings cannot become the focus simply because they are great fun.

COACH'S TIP

Keep it simple! Integrate the stuff of life and Father's stuff.
Never separate the sacred and the secular.
Your paradigm must be shifted to reflect this truth. Then,
whether you are with two or two thousand, you no longer rely
upon some manmade structure, but upon Him and Him alone.
Father's heartbeat remains the same:

". . . where two or three come together in my name,
there am I with them"
Matthew 18:19

Chapter 7

WHO IS THE LEADERSHIP?

BIBLICAL LEADERSHIP

True spiritual leadership is so simple that corrupted hearts cannot see it. For generations the "leaders" among the Called Out Ones have messed it up until it has become a convoluted mass of pagan notions paraded as the will of Father. Read the following verses a couple of times and meditate upon Jesus' words:

> *Jesus called them together and said, "You know that the*
> *rulers of the Gentiles **lord it over them**,*
> *and their high officials **exercise authority over them**.*
> ***Not so with you**. Instead, whoever wants to become*
> *great among you must be your servant,*
> *and whoever wants to be first **must be your slave**—*
> *just as the Son of Man did not come to be served,*
> *but to serve, and to give his life as a ransom for many."*
> Matthew 20:25-28 (Bold mine)

Notice these important phrases:

1. *Lord it over.* Strong's defines it this way: "1) to bring under one's power, to subject one's self, to subdue, master; 2) to hold in subjection, to be master of, exercise lordship over."
2. *Exercise authority over.* This means to wield power over someone else.
3. *Not so with you.* This means "that ain't the way you should do it."
4. *Must be your slave.* Slaves never tell the one they serve what to do. Who has ever heard of such an absurd concept: The servant subduing, mastering, or wielding power over his master?

The hierarchical church system is quite simply a heathen concept!

One verse that typifies the institutional hold upon the Body of Christ is Hebrews 13:17 KJV. Because King James of England oversaw the translation of the text into English, it appears from this, and similar verses throughout the New Testament that he sought to reinforce the hierarchal king-serf system that served his earthly kingdom so well. Look at the tilting of the text toward clergy control:

> *"Obey them that have the rule over you,*
> *and submit yourselves."*

The actual Greek text is better translated: *"Be inclined to be persuaded by those who guide you."*

What is the difference?

"Obey" is a no-nonsense command as opposed to the more relational *"be inclined to be persuaded by."* It simply means that *"those who guide you"* should be given the courtesy of your attention since they are older in the faith, possessing experience and wisdom outside your purview.

The word *"rule"* is likewise domineering and forceful. However, Father's true intention is that the elders—the gray haired—among us should point the way, leading through modeling as opposed to commanding and ruling. This is the intention of Paul's encouragement: *"Therefore I urge you to imitate me"* (1 Corinthians 4:16). He lived his life as a guide for others. In what was this spiritual authority rooted? Look at the verse preceding it. He has established his relationship with them, calling them *"dear children"* and confirming that he is their spiritual father.

PARENTING THE CALLED OUT ONES

So the first question is this: What is true leadership and how does it work? The simplest way to determine how to lead is to think about how the institutional world works and do the opposite. Here are some practical thoughts for life outside the institution.

Do not lord your authority over anyone. That just means: do not tell people what to do. Create a relationship with them that reflects *guide*, the father or mother in the faith, as opposed to *leader*. Parenting embodies the true authority structure to be followed among the Called Out Ones. The joyful part of parenting is the fleeting nature of that authority. The pinnacle of authority occurs when the child is small. The new parent quickly learns that his/her control decrescendos incrementally from the moment the child takes his first breath. As the child grows, he progresses toward greater and greater independence until he becomes your adult peer. Although you remain his father or mother forever, the relationship is constantly evolving. By the time he becomes an adult, he should be able to think for himself and make his own decisions.

Good parents learn the value of guiding as opposed to ruling over their children. When they are very young, decisions must be made for them—for their own good. But skillful parenting is learning to release the decision-making process incrementally throughout the child's life so that by the time he is grown, he can think outside his narrow worldview. He is then prepared to leave the nest and make a nest of his own.

No parent wants his/her thirty-year-old kid to still be living at home. No one wants to be feeding him and changing his diapers for the rest of his life. Yet the institution functions in exactly this way. Thirty years after being born again, church members are expected to eat only the spiritual food served by the spiritual pastor-daddy. They are not allowed to make any decisions on their own. They are told what to think, how to dress, how to worship, and how to raise their earthly children. They are taught to submit to the pastor-daddy because they must always be fed like newborns.

This is the core of the dysfunction among the Saints.

GRAY HAIR

Over the past decade or more, Father's plan for the Western Called Out Ones has been in full operation. He has been preparing the family atmosphere into which the Escapees will find refuge. A large percentage of Saints escaping the traditional church chains are those with gray hair. We are astonished when we meet with groups who want guidance in their new adventure: most of them are middle-aged or older! The revelation that the church system doesn't work seems to come more naturally to them. Spending decade after decade in the institution has brought the older ones to the understanding that it just doesn't work. For all the hype and empty promises, the institution simply does not fulfill the mandates of the Great Commission, nor does it meet the needs of its members. Those who have been subjected to lifelong disappointments are disillusioned by their experience. And they are coming out of the traditional church structure in large numbers.

While it is true that they are disillusioned, Father is using what the enemy has meant for evil for the good of His new move. The Holy Spirit is brooding over the Western Called Out Ones, preparing for a new creation no less remarkable than the one recorded in Genesis. This new race is being created within hearts fully devoted to the Father.

A new atmosphere is being established, and the first parents are being recreated out of the corpse of religiosity.

Father is using the corpse of the church, forming His new family out of what has died. The former incarnation of "church" has been destroyed through emotional hurt and spiritual abuse. From the crucible of Father's presence fathers and mothers of the faith are emerging, tested, destroyed, yet remade into the parents of new generations of Called Out Ones.

We are already seeing the fruit of this first wave toward the Promised Land. There are groups of all ages gathering in diverse ways to worship the King and to fellowship with one another. The future is bright for Father's plan among the Called Out Ones.

PREMATURE BABIES

In this Promised Land outside the institution, you should find folks older in the Lord who have been transformed by His love. He has planned this strategy down to the last detail, so they are around you somewhere. Once you have located them, remember that they are to be your guides, not your pastors. They are not tasked with telling you what to do. That's the control system of the institution. The new elders will not treat you like you're ignorant, but will demand you pursue Father and become mature. In more specific terms: they will enable you to grow up!

The programs of the traditional church structure, by their very nature, are relegated to the lowest common denominator. Since there are always babies being born into the Kingdom family, that denominator is the spiritual baby. Because of this, the pastor must gear the majority of the church programs toward these babies. This has been a problem from the beginning:

> *"We have much to say about this, but it is hard to explain because you are slow to learn. In fact, though by this time you ought to be teachers, you need someone to teach you the elementary truths of God's word all over again. You need milk, not solid food! Anyone who lives on milk, being still an infant, is not acquainted with the teaching about righteousness. But solid food is for the mature, who by constant use have trained themselves to distinguish good from evil."*
> Hebrews 5:11-14

Apparently, the institutionalization of the Saints was in full swing by the time the book of Hebrews was written. The folks who received this letter were out on their own, away from the constant teachings of the Apostles. They began organizing and sterilizing the teachings of Jesus by not pressing one another toward maturity. Humans are notoriously lazy. We want others to tell us what to do and how to do it. It is uncomfortable to mature. It is easy to let Mom and Dad pay for the house and the food while we sleep until noon in a bed for which we did not pay. "Growing up" means taking responsibility for one's life, going to work, paying the bills, and suffering the joys and defeats of adulthood.

We don't want to grow up spiritually, either. It's a whole lot of work. Let papa-pastor do it all. After all, that's why we pay him the big *buck*.

The issue here is a wrong view of the salvation process. The Scriptures parallel spiritual birth with natural birth, yet with the development of crusade evangelism, preaching to the lost with emotional manipulation pressures them to make an immediate decision. Pushing "the decision" to convert to Christianity allows for no incubation period, resulting in thousands, if not millions, of premature spiritual babies.

When does the birth process happen? Is it at the moment the baby's head emerges from the birth canal? Is it when the child first breathes outside the womb?

No.

It begins in intimacy, in a relationship that produces conception. What follows is nine months of swollen ankles, morning sickness, and mood swings. The baby grows from the convergence of seed and egg into a glob of tissue, into a fish-like creature, into a miniature baby, and finally into a viable person prepared for life outside the womb. The labor begins: pain, contractions, and, frankly, a big mess. The water breaks and people are drawn together in anticipation of the emergence of a new member of the family. The baby, now in position with head down, transitions and makes what is always a dramatic entrance into its new environment. Crying is the universal "all-is-well" sign, and then it's off to the races.

Every time you look at this newborn, he's bigger, brighter, and he knows more stuff. Now he can laugh, now he can sit up, then he crawls, followed by the piece de resistance: he starts talking and walking. Then, for the next twenty years he grows steadily into a man.

But, if after all the time and energy and love invested in this man, you still have to spoon-feed him strained prunes, something is drastically wrong. Our expectation is that he will be able to do that for himself, and more, on his own—all in preparation for the time when he will go out and develop an intimate relationship with someone and produce his own children.

However, because the institution is relegated to the lowest common denominator, thirty-year-old saints must be content to exist on whatever comes out of the pastor's blender, strained and pureed for the youngest among us. This is the reason that we have fulfilled this prophecy of the last days:

> *But mark this: There will be terrible times in the last days. People will be lovers of themselves, lovers of money, boastful, proud, abusive, disobedient to their parents, ungrateful, unholy, without love, unforgiving, slanderous, without self-control, brutal, not lovers of the good, treacherous, rash, conceited, lovers of pleasure rather than lovers of God—having a form of godliness but denying its power. Have nothing to do with such people. They are the kind who worm their way into homes and gain control over gullible women, who are loaded down with sins and are swayed by all kinds of evil desires, **always learning but never able to come to a knowledge of the truth**. Just as Jannes and Jambres opposed Moses, so also these teachers oppose the truth. They are men of depraved minds, who, as far as the faith is concerned, are rejected. But they will not get very far because, as in the case of those men, their folly will be clear to everyone.*
> 2 Timothy 3:1-10 (Bold mine)

We are kept as infants being fed by our daddy-pastor year after year, *always learning but never able to come to a knowledge of the truth*. When do we get to graduate from this perpetual pre-school? When do we get to make our own families? We perpetuate dependency and lose out on the thrill, the honor of growing the Kingdom.

It all begins by rushing the birth process of a large percentage of the current population of the Called Out Ones by using emotionally manipulative pleas that tap into people's guilt and fears, inducing them to "pray the prayer and make a decision to receive Christ." This is frequently a forced, premature birth. Instead, it must be the Holy Spirit who draws them, providing the opportunity to have a divine revelation of the risen Christ and compelling them to give their lives fully to Him. Quick fix "fire insurance" does not make disciples of Christ who die daily to self and find intimacy in relationship with their Savior. It frequently produces anemic, dependent souls who live out their lives in the incubator of church life.

INCUBATOR CHRISTIANITY

The traditional church is nothing but an intensive care ward full of incubators with preemies of all ages on life support. Imagine a thirty-year-old jammed into an incubator. She will not know life as it is intended to be. She will not be able to do anything for herself. She needs to be fed rather than having the basic skills needed to feed herself. She will not know the assurance of her salvation. She cannot discover the full extent of her stature since she is confined in someone else's space. She will live her entire life within the confines of that box, never knowing that there is something more.

I contend that the failure of the church can be traced directly to the pews full of premature babies.

My first experience with this phenomenon came with the very first Wednesday evening service I held as a Senior Pastor. It is etched into my memory because of its absurdity. I had prepared a teaching on Psalm 123, *"Behold, as the eyes of servants look unto the hand of their master…"* As part of the discussion, a middle-aged woman raised her hand and asked, "What about God's body?" I was taken aback for a moment, so I asked her to repeat it. "You know, what about God's body? He has a body just like us with arms and legs and everything, right?" She had been in that church for more than twenty five years—teaching Sunday School, sitting on the Governing Board—never coming to an understanding that God is Spirit, without a physical body (see John 4:24). I tossed my teaching aside and started at the very beginning: Who is God? She was as religious as the next person in the pew, but she had never come to any depth of relationship with Father. Not knowing about His body was the tip of her iceberg of ignorance. The Saints in most churches are milk-fed throughout their entire existence, never maturing enough to stand fast in their own faith enough to reproduce another person into the Kingdom.

Consequently, any leadership among the family and clan that meets at your house should look like parenting, celebrating every new understanding, every new depth of relationship with both Father and others in the group. Those parented must understand the goal: mature and get out of your house!

A LEADERSHIP DEVELOPMENT PLAN

Girls and boys begin very early imagining who they will be when they grow up. "I'm going to be a fireman" or "I'm going to be a doctor" are common claims among young children. It is a built-in impulse to grow up and become "someone." The same should be true among the Called Out Ones. I have heard many people say of another, "He has a real call of God on his life," indicating this person shows signs of being elevated to a clergy position.

Actually, we all have the call of God upon our lives:

Now you are the body of Christ, and each one of you is a part of it. And in the church God has appointed first of all apostles, second prophets, third teachers, then workers of miracles, also those having gifts of healing, those able to help others, those with gifts of administration, and those speaking in different kinds of tongues. Are all apostles? Are all prophets? Are all teachers? Do all work miracles? Do all have gifts of healing? Do all speak in tongues? Do all interpret? But

*eagerly desire the greater gifts. And now I will show
you the most excellent way."*
1 Corinthians 12:27-31

We are all called to pull our own weight for the sake of His
Great Name. Grow into maturity yourself, then guide others
through the same treacherous paths over which you have
traveled. Care for the little ones; heal the hurt ones; equip others
to be lovers of Father and His creation; then send them out to
reproduce for the Kingdom.

CARE

Care for them consistently through infancy. If they are
coming out of the traditional church structure, they will most
likely be spiritual infants. These should be treated different from
one newly born into the Kingdom family. They will outwardly
appear to be mature, but they will be suffering from "incubator
legs." They may carry a level of religious arrogance for what
they know about the Kingdom. As you care for them, the old
cliché "tough love" must be applied. Here is a simple plan for
effective caring.

Do not do it for them.

Make demands on the spiritual infants to pursue maturity.
If you allow them to come to your home and sit on your couch
week after week without pushing, cajoling, and encouraging
them to participate, they will remain in the religious disease of
"pew-itis." "Pew-itis" is the condition among the sheep whereby
they remain infants for life and sit obtusely in their favorite pew
every week with their mouths open like little birds. They cannot
feed themselves. In fact, they will have left one or more churches
"because we weren't being fed." The solution to this problem is
to teach them to: feed yourself!

Many parents are task-completion-oriented rather than experience-oriented. When they try to teach the child something, it often ends up with the parent taking the task back, "Oh, let me have it. I'll do it myself."

If you want to teach a child to bake a cake, a finished cake is not the goal. Learning is the goal. There must be tolerance of flour all over the kitchen and probably at least one broken egg on the floor. Model the process for them and then get out of the way and let them do it. If you are the guide of a group of Called Out Ones, show them how, and then sit down. Will they mess it up? Of course! But Father is sovereign over all that, and He will quickly clean up the disarray.

Press them toward independence.

Foment the fledgling desire in spiritual toddlers to move on without you. A good guide will point the way and then get out of the way. Show them how to pray and let them pray. Show them how to teach and let them teach. Show them how to prophesy and then let them do it. Teach them how to do deliverance and let them set others free.

Guides should have enough relationship with the Called Out Ones to operate as a coach as they do their works of service. A coach can say things like, "OK, maybe you should try it this way." Your motivation is to make them better, that is, more of a benefit to the Kingdom. Just remember, coaches don't play; they equip and empower those who play to play better.

Train learners to rely less and less upon your help until they are fully independent. At this point, you become adult peers. Mutual submission is the name of the game. This relationship is to be no longer teacher-pupil but person-to-person.

Bruises are one consequence of the journey to independence. If you want the child to walk without relying upon you to carry him everywhere, then he must endure falling down. As our grandchildren learn to walk, near disaster ensues. They have bruises on their foreheads and under the chin, along with both knees. But instead of giving up, their parents continue to encourage them to persevere. Soon, they are walking experts, finding all sorts of new places to discover.

Press them to make their own "family."
The Called Out Ones within the institution are typically barren. They have been effectively neutered by the religious system. It is widely known that only about two percent of believers ever bring another person into the Kingdom throughout their entire spiritual life. Reproduction must be the goal for all Kingdom family members.

Growing spiritual toddlers should play the daddy and mommy roles of the Kingdom family as they mature so that these skills are honed by repetition and your loving guidance. In the end, they should be sent out to build their own family and clan and tribe.

HEAL

The second part of leadership development is healing. Heal Escapees of the wounds from their past, from spiritual abuse, and from the rigors of life on this planet. Every person coming out of the institution will require deliverance. Since they have lived under the influence of the "dark angel" of religion, they must be set free from any demonic attachment. As they enter the journey to wholeness following deliverance, come alongside them and coach them to grapple with their issues. Sermons have not cured them. This type of relational adventure will.

EQUIP

Equip Escapees in the practical areas of care for others. One of the most important is how to develop relationship with those who are not yet Called Out Ones. Because the traditional church has involuntarily sterilized the vast majority of Saints sitting in the pews, most are incapable of bearing spiritual children. The pastor is the hired-gun responsible for all the reproducing. The programs and activities are focused inward for the comfort of the sheep, so even though there is a constant dripping of guilt to go out and win souls, actual control is never relinquished for it to really happen.

Practical tools for service must be put in place. Teach toddlers how to lay hands on someone and release the presence of Father. Provide relentless practice in study of the Word of God. Teach them to grapple with precepts instead of feeding them. This is accomplished through a simple philosophy: seldom make a definitive statement when teaching in a small group. Instead, ask questions that guide learners to their own revelation. The reason sermons are mostly worthless long term (researchers say that after two hours almost everyone has forgotten what the sermon was even about) is that it is the teacher's revelation, not the hearer's. But when you get down from the pulpit and encourage grappling with the Scriptures, when the precept is grasped it becomes their revelation. And that cannot be so quickly dismissed from their mind.

Teach fathers to lead their families. Teach mothers to do the same. Develop fellowship with one another. And together, pursue Father.

SEND

Send learners out to declare the good news throughout their ethnos, that is, the people within their realm of influence. From the very first moment you begin meeting together, talk about the day when they will be prepared to move out of your house into their own. I have often heard that "there is no such thing as spiritual grandchildren." Phooey! If the natural family is designed to create family lines, so too is the spiritual family. Paul and John, among others, frequently called people "my dear children." So, if your spiritual children reproduce another generation of Called Out Ones then they are your spiritual grandchildren. Every person you reproduce will produce another until that single act of joyful obedience affects many generations of spiritual children as yet unborn.

COACH'S TIP

Create an atmosphere of grace where mistakes can be made. Let leaners be themselves. Don't create clones of yourself. Grow up. Grow them up. And then get them out of your house!

". . . until we all reach unity in the faith and in the knowledge of the Son of God and become mature, attaining to the whole measure of the fullness of Christ. Then we will no longer be infants, tossed back and forth by the waves, and blown here and there by every wind of teaching and by the cunning and craftiness of men in their deceitful scheming. Instead, speaking the truth in love, we will in all things grow up into him who is the Head, that is, Christ.
Ephesians 4:13-15

Chapter 8

DON'T WE NEED A COVERING?

THE COVERING

Outside the institutional church system, each Called Out One gets to experience the joy and terror of self-responsibility. For people who have been spoon-fed for their entire spiritual lives, this will be a challenge, to say the least.

Fear is the normal response.

One of the first queries leveled at Escapees is this: "Who is your covering?" When asked this question, I recommend some variation of the following. Tilt your head to one side, let an innocent, sort of "deer-in-the-headlights" look wash over your face and quip, "Why, Jesus, of course." Your interrogator will probably just leave you alone. The perceived need for a human spiritual covering is often used to guilt people into keeping them under clergy control. The whole idea of "the covering" is a perversion of 1 Corinthians 11:3-7:

> *"Now I want you to realize that the head of every*
> *man is Christ, and the head of the woman is man, and*
> *the head of Christ is God. Every man who prays or*
> *prophesies with his head covered dishonors his head.*
> *And every woman who prays or prophesies with her*

*head uncovered dishonors her head—it is just as though
her head were shaved. If a woman does not cover her
head, she should have her hair cut off; and if it is a
disgrace for a woman to have her hair cut or shaved
off, she should cover her head. A man ought not to
cover his head, since he is the image and glory of God;
but the woman is the glory of man."*

These verses reveal the true spiritual hierarchy: God is the
head of Christ, Christ is the head of man, and man is the head of
his wife. The word "woman" is used here instead of the better
word "wife" in order to exercise heathen control over women,
ensuring that they remain in their place: property. However, in
Christ there is no difference among the Called Out Ones:

*"You are all sons of God through faith in Christ Jesus,
for all of you who were baptized into Christ
have clothed yourselves with Christ.
There is neither Jew nor Greek, slave nor free,
male nor female, for you are all one in Christ Jesus.
If you belong to Christ, then you are Abraham's seed,
and heirs according to the promise."*
Galatians 3:26-29

Father is the headship covering over Christ. Jesus is identified
here as *"Christ"* to indicate his relationship with Father during
his earthly ministry. What did that relationship look like? Father
kept him **safe**; He kept him **secure**, protecting him from harm;
He **comforted** Him; and they fellowshipped in **intimate** love and
adoration. The product of this relationship is that Christ—fully
man and fully God—is exalted to the Father's right hand, a place
of intimacy and authority.

Christ is the headship covering over the man. What does that
relationship look like? Jesus Christ keeps him safe; He keeps

him secure, protecting him from harm; He comforts Him; and they fellowship in intimate love and adoration. The product of this headship relationship is that the man is exalted into a place of intimacy and authority:

> *"The Spirit himself testifies with our spirit that we are*
> *God's children. Now if we are children, then we are*
> *heirs—heirs of God and co-heirs with Christ,*
> *if indeed we share in his sufferings in order*
> *that we may also share in his glory"*
> Romans 8:16-17

We are children of God and heirs of His Kingdom. Remarkable! So, if the relationships between Father and Jesus, and Jesus and man are about safety, security, comfort, and intimate fellowship, what should characterize the headship covering between a man and his wife? Clearly, he must provide safety, protection, comfort, and intimacy for her, as well. Therefore, the additional level of covering is a delightful privilege, as opposed to the "Where's my dinner?" "I'm the head of this house" attitude of the domineering husband as he rules over his wife.

Watch the end product of each relationship: Exaltation! Christ was lifted into the highest place of intimacy and authority possible as a result of Father's covering. Man is lifted into a position of incredible exaltation as a result of his relationship with Christ. Therefore, it must follow that the wife should find herself moving in exalted levels of intimacy and spiritual authority with her husband, with Jesus, and with Father as a result of her relationships.

Single women often ask, "What about me? I have no husband to provide a covering." Jesus is the covering over us, male and female. You just don't have a man in the mix who might mess it all up. Jesus is your covering! When sharing this with groups of Called Out Ones, I usually say it like this: "You don't have some silly man over you, that can mess it up," and generally a cheer arises among the single ladies upon hearing this good news!

DISHONORING YOUR HEAD

Man dishonors his head (Christ) if he allows another man to be his headship covering. The institution is causing a younger brother to stumble in the arena of spiritual authority when it requires submission to a congregational, denominational, or pastoral covering. Jesus is our covering. We need no man, no human priest to stand between us and Father. Jesus fills the bill exquisitely: *"For there is one God and one mediator between God and men, the man Christ Jesus"* (1 Timothy 2:5).

When you submit to another man's headship, you nullify the work of Christ upon the cross, and actually bring *dishonor* upon your Head: Christ!

Therefore, here is an urgent recommendation for life in your Promised Land: never come under another person's spiritual covering (with the exception of wives). Moreover, if you are the guide among a small group of Called Out Ones, refuse— vehemently!— to allow other people to come under your authority or covering.

We are frequently asked this question: "Can we bring our group under your covering, under your authority?" I usually reply, "No. Never." I love to see the startled look on the faces of the poor sheep when it appears that they have been rejected. I follow that abrupt response with a smile and an explanation: "We will serve you in any way you require. We will do so not from above, i.e., serving as the covering over you, but from below. The servant is below, never over or above. This is not my ministry. It is *Jesus'* ministry, and He is the covering over all of us."

Do not allow yourself to control other people, even if they demand it. Come alongside them in their adventure without exercising control or manipulation. Never usurp Christ's authority over others. Empower them to exercise *His* authority in their own lives.

ANOTHER MAN IN THE BED

When a husband allows a pastor or other leader to be the headship covering over his wife, the bonds of intimacy are breached. It is tantamount to bringing another man into your bed! The covering is the most intimate relationship possible between two people. It goes far beyond anything sexual. It is the very definition of intimacy: to *know* another. Breaches in the sacred marriage bed are the root causes of the high divorce rate among the Called Out Ones, and our blind obsession with pastoral authority lend to the dysfunction.

Escapees: don't buy back into such dysfunction! I recommend you renew your marriage vows before the Saints and, husbands, learn to cover your wife and set her free to be exalted beyond your wildest imaginations.

Have you ever wondered why church has traditionally attracted mostly women and children? Men subconsciously know that the institutional system strips them of their God-given authority over their families. The thought of relinquishing authority to another man is repugnant. As a result, they just refuse to go.

Interestingly, we have discovered that the percentage of men within the ranks of Escapees whom we have met in home group meetings and conferences is about equal with the number of women.

Whether you are a man or a woman, Jesus is your covering. Don't make it complicated. Press upward into His presence and discover who He is in you.

He provides remarkable companionship on the adventure.

COACH'S TIP

Jesus is your covering. If you are submitted to another's covering, break that bond immediately, both in the natural and in the spirit realm. Take up the reins of spiritual authority over yourself and your family.

"Therefore let us leave the elementary teachings about Christ and go on to maturity."
Hebrews 6:1

Chapter 9

What Do We Do About Money?

Sticky, Sticky, Sticky

Now we come to the stickiest of the sticky subjects: *money.* To attempt to touch one's money in our culture is to poke at the very heart of our national god. Numerous Escapees exhibit fundraising fatigue from the myriad of projects proposed by ministries. Many are suspicious; most are confused.

Once again, you must make a mature determination for yourself while listening to the Holy Spirit. I will give some snippets of thought to help guide you toward finding Father's heart regarding what "giving" looks like outside the traditional church structure.

Is Tithing For Today?

Often, pundits of the house church movement gravitate to one extreme or another when addressing the topic of the tithe. On the one hand, some teach that tithing is an Old Testament precept, having no place in the life of a New Testament Called Out One. On the other hand, the institutional propaganda machine—so committed to taking our money to fund their vision—has made tithing the source of so much guilt and condemnation many Saints dare not miss one tithe payment since they might be *"rob*[bing] *God"* (See Malachi 3:10), thus incurring a curse upon their finances.

Some Escapee writers are adamant that tithing is obsolete.

The basis for this philosophy is founded in Scriptures like *"Let everyone give as his heart tells him. There should be no pain or sense of compulsion"* (2 Corinthians 9:7). This is usually followed by an overview of New Testament references proclaiming that everything is the Lord's, not just ten percent. While this is doctrinally admirable on its face, I think it misses the true nature of our Jewish roots and robs us of a fundamental joy regarding the tithe. Additionally, without a giving target, many not only do not even give ten percent, but also fail to give at all when the opportunity presents itself.

The other extreme is represented by those who hold to the tithe as it is presented, or as it is purportedly presented, under the Mosaic Law. Some of our friends are so under the bondage of tithing that they are unable to discover the true joy of the *"cheerful giver"* aspect of giving under grace. They have been indoctrinated in institutional thinking and follow that teaching religiously.

I think there is a better way.

A UNIVERSAL PRINCIPLE

I am convinced that the principle of tithing is as universal on planet earth as the law of gravity. It functions in the earthly realm whether we acknowledge it or not. Many ungodly business people use tithing to unlock blessing upon their businesses even though they do not acknowledge the One who established the principle. It is also a basic corporate success strategy taught in business seminars. It is a principle of the universe established for our benefit.

The tithe transcends the Old Covenant, that is, it occurred before the Law was established, was incorporated into the Mosaic Law, and remains in effect under the New Covenant. The first appearance of tithing is found in Genesis 14 and is referenced in Hebrews 7:

> *"This Melchizedek was king of Salem and priest of God Most High. He met Abraham returning from the defeat of the kings and* **blessed him,** *and Abraham gave him a tenth of everything."*
> Hebrews 7:1-2 (Bold mine)

Two things are significant here. First, Melchizedek was a priest before the Mosaic Law and was therefore free of the constraints of the Law. Second, the atmosphere surrounding the tithe was exclusively blessing. Melchizedek blessed Abraham and Abraham reciprocated by blessing him with the tithe. Only under the Mosaic Law was the curse added to the concept of tithing (see Malachi 3). The tenth produces blessing for the giver as well as the recipient (notice the bold portion of the verse above).

Now that the New Covenant is in effect, the curse has been removed and the environment of blessing once again dominates the subject of the tithe. The New Testament does not mention the command contained in the Law, but puts stress on the relational aspects of giving. It is therefore perfectly compatible with the underlying precepts of fellowship with God and fellowship with one another that undergird New Testament theology.

The curse associated with the tithe has been removed. The curse originated in the Law to show the shortcomings of the Israelites: *"You are under a curse—the whole nation of you—because you are robbing me"* (Malachi 3:9). However, when the work of the Cross was completed, the curse was removed and blessing reemerged: *"Christ redeemed us from the curse of the law by becoming a curse for us, for it is written: 'Cursed is everyone who is hung on a tree'"* (Galatians 3:13). Therefore, giving can be both cheerful and targeted without turning it into some arbitrary rule we follow because we fear attracting a curse upon our finances.

THE FLOODGATES OF BLESSING

Therefore, a new reality is revealed. The tenth opens the doorway to blessing:

> *"Bring the whole tithe into the storehouse, that there may be food in my house. Test me in this," says the Lord Almighty, and see if I will not **throw open the floodgates of heaven and pour out so much blessing that you will not have room enough for it"***
> Malachi 3:10 (Bold mine)

Ten percent should be the basic target of our giving. It provides us with the necessary seed to expect a harvest of blessing in our finances, the first step in the process toward financial blessing. However, that step is only the beginning of cheerful giving.

Once the initial giving goal is met, we may have an expectation of blessing upon our finances and protection from the ravages of the Enemy's thieving ways. Planting more seed will produce a greater harvest.

THE RECIPIENTS OF OUR GIVING

Since the institution has always pilfered the financial blessings of the people to fund their own vision, we must submit to another paradigm shift now that we are set free to give as Father intended. Our intention is to be of the greatest benefit to the Called Out Ones and those who may join us.

The tithe has a specific function. From the very first occurrence of the tithe through the dark days of the Mosaic Law and therefore today, the tithe must be given to meet the needs of people. A tithe given to finance a building program does not open the blessing door. Offerings are for just such purposes. The tithe must be given to people. Even under the Old Covenant, the tithe was given to meet the needs of the people, to feed them, to meet their personal needs. Abraham did not give into Melchizedek's treasury. The tenth was given to the man. When the Tabernacle and the Temple were built, offerings were received, not tithes. Every instance of giving in the New Testament is targeted toward meeting the needs of people. Certainly, any giving above this threshold is an offering and can bless buildings, and other projects.

So, who are these people for whom the tithe was intended?

The Poor

Closest to Father's heart in the matter of giving are the poor. Many allowances were made for the poor under the Old Covenant: *He who is kind to the poor lends to the Lord, and he will reward him for what he has done* (Proverbs 19:17). Throughout the New Testament, the Saints consistently gave to the poor: *All they asked was that we should continue to remember the poor, the very thing I was eager to do* (Galatians 2:10).

Escapees must make giving to the poor a priority. In modern times, we have abdicated this responsibility to the government. But there is a segment of our society falling through the cracks of the Welfare system: the working poor. These are people who do not rely on government entitlements. They work hard to feed their families, but find it difficult, if not impossible, to make ends meet. I recommend that Escapees bless these wonderful people whenever possible.

There are many groups serving the poor across the world who certainly deserve our financial attention. Find them, develop relationships with them, and give as you like. Blessing will surely follow.

The Widows and the Fatherless

No less vital to Father's heart are the widows and the fatherless. In first century society men in their thirties married teenage women. Thus, there were many widows whose husbands died of old age while the woman was still relatively young. Consequently, the early Called Out Ones were tasked with caring for a large population of widows: *"Religion that God our Father accepts as pure and faultless is this: to look after orphans and widows in their distress and to keep oneself from being polluted by the world"* (James 1:27).

In our culture, the same condition exists, though the formula is different. We call them single parents. They are husband-less women, modern widows. Most of us have some in our own families, in addition to those at work or in our communities. In many cases, giving may take the form of our time and energy to help them around their homes or with their children. In any case, widows are everywhere and are in need.

With the divorce rate skyrocketing, children are often left without balanced influences. Make them part of your family and share your blessings with them. Befriending single parent families provides many opportunities to meet personal needs of the fatherless. Money, time and attention are equally vital to their lives. Give all of them.

The Itinerants

Although there is no indication from Scripture that pastors or teachers received their living from their ministries, there is a place for itinerant servants to receive their living from the Called Out Ones. Apparently, apostles, prophets, and evangelists who declared the Good News were to be financed by those who were inclined to share in their ministry: *"In the same way, the*

Lord has commanded that those who preach the gospel should receive their living from the gospel" (1 Corinthians 9:14). From both Scripture and early Called Out Ones' writings, we find that those who remained in a specific locale worked their own jobs and served without payment. However, traveling apostolic teams would stop by the gatherings to impart spiritual wisdom or provide teaching on specific subjects and were cared for by the local Saints. The elders did not receive salaries from those who met at their houses. They were simply business people or farmers who agreed to guide others in the Way.

Today, apostolic teams are as active as in the First Century and are prime candidates for financial help. They bring their teaching or training to local groups of Called Out Ones and are supported by those who desire to take part in their itinerant ministries.

Included in these itinerant groups are those who make short-term missions trips. In recent years the number of available missions opportunities have grown exponentially. It is perfectly proper to give to someone who is going to serve the Saints in another country, whether short term or permanently. In fact, it is a grand opportunity to use your tithe to fund your own missions trip since we know that, under the Old Covenant, the yearly trip to the Temple was funded by the tithe.

In any event, the tithe may be used to meet the needs of traveling teams who build the Called Out Ones.

WHAT ABOUT MY TAX RECEIPT?

Even the smallest gathering of saints may call themselves a "church" and receive tax-deductible donations. The Internal Revenue Service recognizes that small groups tend to grow into institutional churches, so check with an accountant or lawyer and get advise as how to protect yourself and your group.

But as far as giving to the poor, or to others who may not in any way be construed as a "church," I offer three little words: Let it go! There is nothing wrong with getting a tax receipt for your giving, however, it tends to restrict to whom you want to give since your focus may be upon the tax benefits as opposed to the simple obedience of giving when a need arises: *He who is kind to the poor lends to the Lord, and he will reward him for what he has done* (Proverbs 19:17). Many have exchanged the blessing of the *floodgates of heaven* (see Malachi 3:10) for minuscule tax relief. Luke 6:30 hits this point marvelously: *Give to everyone who asks you.*

Simple, clean, and doable.

So, don't worry about the tax receipt:

"Do not store up for yourselves treasures on earth, where moth and rust destroy, and where thieves break in and steal. But store up for yourselves treasures in heaven, where moth and rust do not destroy, and where thieves do not break in and steal. For where your treasure is, there your heart will be also"
Matthew 6:19-21

THE PARABLE OF THE MOOSE

The days of building church buildings in the name of the Lord are gone. If we had used the funds invested in real estate over the past two thousand years for the actual work of the Kingdom, I wonder how many more Called Out Ones would be among us today. Church buildings are monuments to the men who build them, nothing more. Our tithes have been used to build them, thus robbing us of the intended blessing.

Tithes used to pay the light bill are as dead as those used to build the building. This sort of expense must be paid by offerings over and above the tithe so as not to thwart the intended blessing on the tithe.

As this revelation dawned on me, the Lord showed me the absurdity of my colleagues' claims that Father had answered their prayers and provided the funds to build Him a building.

The local chapter of the Moose Club owned a building down the road from my house. They decided that it was time for a new building. As I watched it being built, the Lord asked me, "How did they build this building?" I responded, "They organized a fundraising committee, sold bonds, borrowed money, and soon, a new building was built." The whole project came off very smoothly. The new building was bright and clean and it attracted new members to come to socialize.

Then He asked, "How do my children build their buildings?" The answer was obvious: "They organize a fundraising committee, sell bonds, borrow money, and soon, a new building is built. The only difference is the church says that the Lord did it. But if the same group were Moose, they could accomplish the very same thing without You."

"That's why you aren't allowed to build Me a building."

Just because you can do it doesn't mean Father was involved. Church buildings are a waste of money. Sell them and use the money to build an orphanage or a hospital, or to feed the poor. As much as you will be tempted to build your own church building as your house group grows, don't do it. Split the group and send them out to gather others into the harvest.

EVERYTHING BELONGS TO THE LORD

It is clear that everything is truly Father's. Make the tithe your jumping off point and give more just for fun. It does not have to go to the same people all the time. Keep your money in your pocket and watch where Father wants you to give. I have many friends who keep their tithe with them, joyfully observing the world through Father's eyes, waiting for Him to show them to whom they should give. Great joy is derived through seeing your gifts benefit people. Find deinstitutionalized ways to give, and you will experience giggles in the process.

COACH'S TIP

Shake the institutional paradigms of giving and discover the pleasure of making Father happy as your heart beats synchronously with His regarding your money.

"Give, and it will be given to you. A good measure, pressed down, shaken together and running over, will be poured into your lap. For with the measure you use, it will be measured to you."
Luke 6:38

Chapter 10

CAN WOMEN MINISTER?

SILENT BUT DEADLY

Perhaps the most effective part of the lie perpetrated upon the church concerns women in ministry. We have been duped into believing that women are second-class citizens without spiritual authority or ministry among the Called Out Ones. Of course, they can raise the children and the food, but definitely not spiritual food.

This lie is so strong it often makes its way into the gatherings of Escapees. Recently, we were put in contact with a group of Escapees who were contemplating joining a collection of home groups under the oversight of a man from another city. However, they were concerned about his stance on women in ministry. He taught them that *"women should remain silent in the churches"* (1 Corinthians 14:33) to the degree that they couldn't even speak during the fellowship time in the home group.

A few thoughts for your consideration:

1. If women aren't allowed to speak among the Called Out Ones, why did Joel's prophecy include them?

"In the last days, God says, I will pour out my Spirit on

*all people. Your sons and **daughters** will prophesy, your
young men will see visions, your old men will dream
dreams. Even on my servants, both men and **women**, I
will pour out my Spirit in those days,
and they will prophesy."*
Acts 2:17-18 (Bold mine)

2. If women aren't allowed to speak among the Saints, to whom
did the daughters of Phillip prophesy?

*"Leaving the next day, we reached Caesarea and stayed
at the house of Philip the evangelist, one of the Seven.
He had four unmarried daughters who prophesied."*
Acts 21:8-9

3. If women aren't allowed to speak, to whom did the woman
at the well speak when she purportedly witnessed to her whole
village about Jesus?

*"Then, leaving her water jar, the woman went back
to the town and said to the people, 'Come,
see a man who told me everything I ever did.
Could this be the Christ?'"*
Verses 28-29 of John 4:5-29

4. Was Phoebe mute as she served the Called Out Ones?

*"I commend to you our sister Phoebe, a servant of the
church in Cenchrea. I ask you to receive her in the Lord
in a way worthy of the saints and to give her any help
she may need from you, for she has been a great help to
many people, including me."*
Romans 16:1-2

104

5. How does one contend for the faith without speaking?

"Yes, and I ask you, loyal yokefellow, help these women who have contended at my side in the cause of the gospel, along with Clement and the rest of my fellow workers, whose names are in the book of life."
Philippians 4:3

6. Did Anna use sign language to prophesy to Joseph and Mary?

*"There was also a **prophetess**, Anna, the daughter of Phanuel, of the tribe of Asher. She was very old; she had lived with her husband seven years after her marriage, and then was a widow until she was eighty-four. She never left the temple but worshiped night and day, fasting and praying. Coming up to them at that very moment, she gave thanks to God **and spoke** about the child to all who were looking forward to the redemption of Jerusalem."*
Luke 2:36-38 (Bold mine)

7. How could Paul consider Junias an apostle if she could not speak? (The word "Junias" was originally feminine. Male scribes made the change to the masculine to maintain the stranglehold they had over the women, keeping them in their place.)

"Greet Andronicus and Junias, my relatives who have been in prison with me. They are outstanding among the apostles, and they were in Christ before I was."
Romans 16:7

8. Did these women elders serve while not speaking?

Mary

> *"When this had dawned on him, he went to the house*
> *of Mary the mother of John, also called Mark, where*
> *many people had gathered and were praying."*
> Acts 12:12

Lydia

> *"After Paul and Silas came out of the prison, they went*
> *to Lydia's house, where they met with the brothers and*
> *encouraged them. Then they left."*
> Acts 16:40

Priscilla and Aquila

> *"Greet Priscilla and Aquila, my fellow workers in*
> *Christ Jesus. They risked their lives for me. Not only I*
> *but all the churches of the Gentiles are grateful to them.*
> *Greet also the church that meets at their house."*
> Romans 16:3-5

Chloe

> *"My brothers, some from Chloe's household have*
> *informed me that there are quarrels among you."*
> 1 Corinthians 1:11

EVIDENCE TO THE CONTRARY

There are several problem passages in the New Testament that are the source of the controversy about women's place in the gathering of the Saints. However, if the verses above are true and the verses that follow seem to contradict them, then an investigation is warranted to uncover the truth.

Here are the problem passages:

(1)

"A woman should learn in quietness and full submission. I do not permit a woman to teach or have authority over a man; she must be silent."
1 Timothy 2:11-12

Contextually, this verse is addressing a specific problem in Ephesus. Women there were evidently teaching false doctrine. With a little exegesis, we may find a better rendering of this verse that remains true to both the words and the context: *"I am not **presently allowing** (present tense) a woman to teach"* (bold mine).

The imposed silence is therefore discipline for those false teachers as opposed to a blanket doctrinal statement for all women of all time.

(2)

"Women should remain silent in the churches. They are not allowed to speak, but must be in submission, as the Law says. If they want to inquire about something, they should ask their own husbands at home; for it is disgraceful for a woman to speak in the church."
1 Corinthians 14:34-35

If the word "silent" was intended to be a blanket doctrinal statement for all women of all time, then women should not be allowed to teach their children or sing in public worship. It would mean that the women could not be greeters, Sunday School teachers, or do the announcements as part of the liturgy of the institutional church. Nobody likes mimes! So, why do we expect the women to participate only through hand motions?

Apparently the women in Corinth were shouting to their husbands across the room. Remember, in the Middle Eastern culture men and women would not be seated together. Additionally, first century women were rarely educated, so it was natural for them to have many questions. This verse is simply a solution to the problem of several disrupting conversations taking place at once while someone else was talking. Encouraging them to ask their husbands in the privacy of their own homes was a directive to the husbands to educate their wives in the ways of the Lord so that they could understand better when the Called Out Ones dialogued:

(3)
*"And every woman who prays or prophesies with her
head uncovered dishonors her head—it is just as though
her head were shaved."*
1 Corinthians 11:5

The matter of the covering was dealt with in another chapter, but it is important to shed some light on this passage in the context of women in ministry. Middle Eastern culture decreed that women should wear clothes that completely covered them. The custom remains today.

However, I dispute the interpretation of what the covering is. I believe that the context clearly shows that her hair is the sign of the covering as opposed to a hat or veil of some sort. This sign is for spirit beings, as opposed to people. It is not apparent from this passage why women require this extra level of protection. However, it may mean that they are somehow more sensitive to spirit influence and that Father has provided the gift of her husband as a remedy. If you are inclined to make women wear a doily on her head while in worship or teaching, then you have only gone part way. She should wear a burka. The head covering is part of a burka-type costume. Do you think your wife would be comfortable shopping in Wal-Mart covered head to toe in forty pounds of fabric? Certainly, if you want to do it, there will be no argument from me.

Just asking ....

The covering to which Paul refers is a sign of the headship covering of a woman's husband. The real issue is clearly the desire to usurp the covering of the husband, which exposes the wife to dark spiritual influences. The emotionally perceptive and spiritually sensitive nature of the female of the species is too precious a gift to leave exposed. When wives usurp their husband's covering it is nullified and makes them vulnerable to malevolent spiritual influences as is indicated in verse ten of that chapter: *"For this reason, and because of the angels, the woman ought to have a sign of authority on her head"* (1 Corinthians 11:10).

CHAPTER 46 – MODERN EXPERIENCE

Many Western churches lag behind in releasing their women to serve the King. Escapees who retain this dysfunction of the traditional church structure are perpetuating the chains of bondage upon a new generation of Called Out Ones. I join with Paul when he said: *"It is for freedom that Christ has set us free. Stand firm, then, and do not let yourselves be burdened again by a yoke of slavery"* (Galatians 5:1).

If you stifle the voices of women in your gatherings, then I submit that you are still captive to the male-dominated, clergy-dominated, institutional paradigm. First, husbands, cover your wives so that they can explore the realms of the Spirit at ease and with confidence. Then, set them free to prophesy, evangelize, pray, sing, and teach within the vast expanses of their giftings.

All are one in Christ Jesus!

"You are all sons of God through faith in Christ Jesus, for all of you who were baptized into Christ have clothed yourselves with Christ. There is neither Jew nor Greek, slave nor free, male nor female, for you are all one in Christ Jesus."
Galatians 3:26-28

Coach's Tip

Women of God, you have escaped the grasp of the institution, now escape the tyranny of sexism
by submitting to the headship covering of your husband, even though it seems upside down!
If you have no husband, remember: Jesus is your covering.
Men of God, release the women around you to minister as you stand watch for their protection. Until then, you will only get part of what Father has for you.

"Submit to one another out of reverence for Christ."
Ephesians 5:21

Chapter 11

How Do We Worship?

Worship

In modern church vernacular, "worship" has come to mean a variety of things. Our liturgical ceremonies are called "worship services." Among most denominations, worship means that part of a service where we sing. In reality, music has little to do with worship. Certainly, it may be used as a vehicle to proclaim praise or worship, but it is not a necessary component for a worship experience.

A Paradigm Shift

Those who have experienced a steady diet of CD-quality worship music in Sunday morning services in institutional churches find it very difficult to make the transition to true worship. Frequently, they lament, "What will we do about worship? We need worship."

Indeed.

Discovering the biblical pattern for true "worship" is a simple exercise available to anyone with a Hebrew-English lexicon. Throughout the Old Testament there are about a hundred words relating to worship and praise of the Living God. The issue is not *where* to find the atmosphere for worship, but *how* to become a *worshipper*.

A Hebrew professor once shared an interesting Hebrew word with his class. The Hebrew word *avodah* may be translated "worship." It may also be translated "study of the Torah (the Word of God)," as well as "work."

It is not surprising that study of the Word is considered an act of worship. However, that "work" might be considered worship is an entirely different matter. The work you do every day is an act of worship to Father: *"So whether you eat or drink or whatever you do, do it all for the glory of God"* (1 Corinthians 10:31). We eat for His glory; we drink for His glory; we work and play and do laundry for His glory.

Escapees, if you can get this revelation for yourself, it will change your life. How would your work environment change if you were completely convinced that every paper you shuffled, or every nail you drove, was intended to bring glory to Father? How would the atmosphere of your house change if those messy diapers represented your acknowledgment of His glory?

Mowing the lawn would no longer be such drudgery since you are offering it as worship to your Creator. These actions are as essential to your worship experience as dancing in front of a ten-foot-high stack of speakers blasting the latest praise band.

So, ask the question again, "How do we worship?" Constantly. And with conviction.

WORSHIP MUSIC

My daughter Erin is an accomplished musician. She is, more importantly, a worshipper. She writes songs of worship and offers them to Father in adoration. She has learned to use her voice as a gift of worship and leads groups before the Lord in praise. But it is not just her music that exudes worship. Her very life is an act of worship and praise. Music is just one part of the whole worship experience.

There is nothing corrupt or wrong about using the vehicle of music to ride into His presence. The difficulty arises when that is the *only* expression you offer. You should develop your worshipping lifestyle in everything you do so that when you get an opportunity to gather with other Called Out Ones to express your heart to Father, you may do so with gusto.

The appearance of choirs was the first step on the slippery slope to institutional control over music. Choirs were hired to sing for the people, since the people could not be expected to acceptably perform. The clergy robbed us of this expression of celebration.

A couple of thousand years later, the majority of Saints do not participate when such worship experiences are held. Why? Because we still don't sound good enough; our voices are not offered with professional quality. I think the ability to record sound has been the greatest deterrent to the full worship music experience since Emperor Constantine employed the choirs from the heathen temples to replace group singing.

I hear this lament everywhere we go, "I can't sing." Is it that you cannot sing? Or is it that you feel that you just don't measure up to others and are therefore disqualified from bringing your sacrifice of praise to Father?

Even as recent as fifty years ago, families would gather on special occasions and sing together, maybe around a piano or other instrument, but frequently without the help of any instruments whatsoever. Taverns were a place of social gathering but, maybe to your surprise, they did not have a jukebox. The people sat around enjoying one another's company, singing what we have come to know as drinking songs. Interestingly, many of the now-sacred hymns of the church were simply drinking tunes from the taverns with different words added, among them Luther's, "A Mighty Fortress Is Our God." Everyone sang. You could howl along and enjoy the experience without being compared to a perfect rendition you once heard on a record.

With the advent of recordings, the standards have grown so stringent that most of the Called Out Ones are reticent to bellow out their joyful noise for fear of embarrassment.

So, sing in the shower. No one is there to shame you, and the acoustics are usually better than in the church building anyway.

Sing loud; sing for joy; sing unto the Lord a new song. Make up the words as an expression of love and adoration for Him.

Little children don't care what they sound like. My granddaughter Isabelle walks around all day long singing her version of one song or another. When she comes to my house, I always ask her, "Do you have a song for grandpa?" She is still too young to have discovered shame, so she simply climbs up on my lap and sings for me. What do you think my heart does? Do I correct her pitch or make sure she says the right words? Of course not! It's not about the performance; it's about the intimacy. This is the very definition of worship.

While in the middle of teaching on worship in a seminar, I looked up and saw a bunch of my grandkids come in the back door. Without hesitation, one by one they made their way around the people and came up to me, arms extended. I took each one into my arms and spent just a moment with them. By the time we were done, a revelation had been given: we had experienced a demonstration of real worship.

PRACTICE

Worship may be defined this way: Being occupied with *who* God is. Praise is being occupied with what God has *done*. It seems easier to praise than to worship because there is still some of us in praise. Worship is a complete focus on Him.

It takes practice.

Are you distractible? I am. My son-in-law Jason always says

that no matter what is happening, all you have to do is shake a shiny object in front of me and you've captured my attention. Worshipping with a whole bunch of people around is difficult for me.

I led a worship team for many years and found that I could not look at the people while doing so. There were all these distractions, people looking at their watches or yawning or staring at the ceiling. If I spent much time watching them, I would get increasingly angry at their nonparticipation.

So, I led music with my eyes closed.

REAL WORSHIP

Music is only one expression of worship. Rick Joyner's Morning Star troops have been experimenting with activities such as painting or sculpting as the musical team plays. It's quite a departure from what is considered the norm and is a step in the right direction.

What if you really have no artistic talent whatsoever?

Offer something during worship, whether in a corporate setting or by yourself, that He considers an act of worship. Certainly, singing and dancing before the Lord brings Him great joy. But within these experiences it is important to utilize the full arsenal of praise and worship actions. I have included a list of worship and praise words that appear in the Old Testament so you can choose whatever makes Father happy and that you can actually do. In our seminars, I always encourage the people to choose something different from the list every time they get into worship. You might do the same. He wrote the Scriptures so the expressions found therein are likely to make Him happy. The words are listed from the most often used to the least. This is not an exhaustive list, but these few will get you started.

1. Hallal – to give forth a joyful shout; to be clamorously foolish
2. Yadah – to worship with extended hands; to throw out the hands in celebration
3. Barak – to bend the knee in salute; to bless
4. Tehellah – to sing a song of praise
5. Zamar – to make music of praise with instruments
6. Giyl – to rejoice; leap for joy; to spin around
7. Todah – a sacrifice of praise; to extend hands in thanksgiving
8. Rua – to shout for joy and triumph; excited, loud, unrestrained praise
9. Rum – to exalt; to celebrate as a victor
10. Kabad – to glorify as awesomely honorable
11. Gadal – to grow larger
12. Shabach – to shout
13. Samach – to make merry
14. Alats – to jump for joy
15. Ranan – a triumphant shout
16. Alac – to wave arms joyfully
17. Zamir – to sing joyfully
18. Hadah – to rejoice
19. Hul – to dance
20. Hillul – a celebration of thanksgiving
21. Haphetz – to delight in
22. Kaved – to honor
23. Maha – to clap
24. Natan – to proclaim
25. Selal – to sing in exaltation
26. Pazaz – to leap
27. Patzah – to burst forth with
28. Paar – to boast
29. Avar – to let resound
30. Raqad – to skip around
31. Tzavad – to cry aloud
32. Nasa – to lift

Make a copy of this list and carry it with you. When you think of Father while in line at the grocery store, I recommend you try number fourteen. Use it in the backyard or when you are at lunch at work. Practice all of them.

I like worshipping while mowing the lawn. The tractor is very loud and it drowns out both my voice and any outside distractions. Keeping my eye on the grass makes it easy to let my mind wander into Father's presence. I talk to Him at the top of my voice or sing made-up songs for His amusement.

Find a place to practice. So what if you sound like someone is strangling a cat? Let it rip! Father's heart swells with joy when we occupy our minds and hearts with Him.

Many Escapees from more conservative traditions find difficulty with such so-called frivolity. But remember, I didn't create these words to foment Charismatic craziness. Father inspired the Word with His idea of worship and praise and the rest of it is for us to obey.

Have fun and try not to pull any muscles.

I'm not much of a dancer. In fact, there should be a law that restricts me from it altogether. During a particularly severe time of depression, I foolishly attended a worship conference at a regional amusement park. There were big tents set up for the workshops, so I shuffled into the back of one. Right off the bat, I didn't like the guy speaking. He seemed too happy. I hated happy.

But I stayed anyway.

Toward the end of his talk, he demanded that we put what he had said into action. I thought, sarcastically, "Oh sure, just watch me!" as he played some inane song on his keyboard, the crowd was bobbing up and down to the beat of the music.

The Holy Spirit spoke to me. He said one word, "Dance."

I knew it was Him because I would never make up something like that. Certainly the devil didn't say it.

117

It had to be Him.

I said out loud, "No."

He said it again, more urgently, "Dance."

Have you ever been in depression? Dancing, if I might be so bold, is probably the furthest thing from your mind when you are under that heavy weight. On a good day, I wasn't about to dance, let alone when I felt like I did at that moment.

"Dance!" he said it again, almost shouting.

I rose to my feet and bobbed up on the balls of my feet a few times.

"There! Are you happy?"

I could almost feel His eyes boring a hole into the back of my head.

"Okay, okay!"

I moved a few of the chairs around me knowing that this was going to be ugly. Thankfully I was in the very back row and everyone else was busy sweating to the oldies.

I gave it a half-hearted jump—there really wasn't going to be anything that remotely resembled dancing—and looked around to see who was laughing at me. Nobody paid any attention.

The moment of truth: Dance or disobey.

I jumped a little higher; I broke a sweat; I jumped higher and with more energy.

Something amazing happened: I smiled, first at my own absurd gyrations, then because I felt better, not physically since I was wheezing and sweating, but because it occurred to me that Father thought it was funny.

Within a matter of minutes, I was jumping around like an idiot.

The depression disappeared. Apparently, it fell to the ground and I stomped all over it while obeying Father.

It might not surprise you that I like number nineteen above, even when I'm not depressed.

PRACTICAL WORSHIP HOW TO'S

1. Get some worship CD's, put them on as loud as you can stand it, and focus your attention on Father. It will take practice, but just do it.
2. Speak words of praise and worship to Him continually. Tell Him what you think of Him.
3. Learn how to play the piano, guitar or the spoons (depending upon your geographical location) and make a joyful noise unto the Lord.
4. When together with other Called Out Ones, start singing a tune from your heart to Father. Make up the words as you go.
5. Get around some preschoolers and put on some hot music. Watch them and do what they do.
6. Study the Word. Read it out loud to Him. Talk to Him about it. Ask Him questions.
7. Again, sell cars or manufacture lawn equipment for His glory. Talk to Him about it. Tell Him that those clean dishes are for His glory.
8. Fire up the barbeque grill, invite the neighbors in, sit around the campfire and tell of His wonders.

A REASONABLE ACT OF WORSHIP

Worship affects the three parts of your being: spirit, soul, and body. You make a spirit-to-Spirit connection with His Holy Spirit. Worship develops the sensitivity to hear His still small voice in the depths of your spirit: *"My sheep hear my voice, and I know them, and they follow me"* (John 10:27 KJV).

The soulish areas of your being are deeply altered by active worship. The three areas of the soul include your mind, your will, and your emotions. Your mind gains focus as you practice concentrating on who He is and what He has done. Distractions move into the shadows as His face occupies the forefront of your

119

attention. Your will is submitted to His as you offer yourself in worship. Your emotions open more fully and the deep hurts are exposed to Him for healing.

Finally, your body, persistently offered as a living sacrifice, is brought more and more under control so that it is less apt to get you into trouble. Notice that every one of the thirty-two words in the list above involves some sort of bodily movement. Paul writes the consummate expression on this subject to the Called Out Ones at Rome:

> *"Therefore, I urge you, brothers, in view of God's mercy, to offer your **bodies** as living sacrifices, holy and pleasing to God—this is your **spiritual** act of worship. Do not conform any longer to the pattern of this world, but be transformed by the renewing of your **mind**. Then you will be able to test and approve what God's **will** is—his good, pleasing and perfect will."*
> Romans 12:1-2 (Bold mine)

Our spiritual act of worship affects the spirit, the soul, and the body. It is your joy to practice your worship until you get to do it face to face in the world to come.

Coach's Tip

Just do it! Say worship; sing worship; move in worship.
Do it now; do it often; do it continually.

> *"Through Jesus, therefore, let us continually offer to God a sacrifice of praise—the fruit of lips that confess his name."*
> Hebrews 13:15

Chapter 12

WHAT DO WE DO NOW?

JUST DO IT

The important thing now is to transform all this theory into practical terms. As a Spectator you were allowed to take it all in and let it turn to spiritual fat. But can't you hear the coach yelling at the top of his lungs: "Get off the couch! If you ain't sweating, you ain't doing it right!"

It's time to do it right.

JOB ONE

As premature babies in the spiritual incubator of the institution, we were deluded into appraising our spiritual state in terms of church attendance, how many Bible verses were memorized, total tithe, or the size of the Bible carried. All that is nice, but it doesn't create a workable plan for healthy, on-going spiritual maturity.

I offer you such a plan.

I am convinced that few among us have a revelation of what a real Called Out One should look like. The externals upon which we formerly relied have come to nothing. The people outside the Body of Christ have little or no interest in becoming one of us— apparently because we look and act so much like them—and they resist the thought of all those rules and the guilt manipulation being compounded upon their already dismal lives.

Job one, then, is to find a model of true Christian living that Jesus can use to *"draw all men unto* [himself]" (John 12:32, brackets mine).

FOUNDATIONS

Newcomers into the body of Christ need to stand upon a firm foundation of the Word of God. Churches use a variety of tools to build this foundation, including Babes in Christ classes, membership classes, baptismal classes, and the like. All of that is well and good, but I contend that such methods leave much to be desired.

Many groups recommend that the new Saint initiate his reading of the Word with the Gospel of John. Here again, I think we miss the point by doing so. While it is important that this gospel be read—and often—the better way is to devour the book of First John. Within its pages are found the clothing of the new believer. This short book reveals the basic modus operandi of Saint concisely and simply, thereby setting the stage for true Christian living.

FELLOWSHIP

When asked which was the greatest Commandment, Jesus replied:

> *"'Love the Lord your God with all your heart and with all your soul and with all your mind.' This is the first and greatest commandment. And the second is like it: 'Love your neighbor as yourself.'"*
> Matthew 22:37-39

Fellowship with Father and fellowship with one another. The whole of Father's plan is wrapped up in this simple phrase. It's all about intimate fellowship both with Father and with one another. As I explained previously, fellowship means literally becoming part of one another. Fellowship with Father is a lifelong pursuit to be enjoyed by every one of His children. We are thrilled to discover who He is as our fellowship grows deeper and richer over the years. However, *the second is like it.*" It is equally important to mature interpersonal relationships with other Called Out Ones within the context of our new life in the Promised Land. Sadly, I don't think the institution is able to meet this challenge.

The atmosphere of the Promised Land must be transformed by this life-altering precept:

> *"Anyone who claims to be in the light but hates his brother is still in the darkness. Whoever loves his brother lives in the light, and there is nothing in him to make him stumble. But whoever hates his brother is in the darkness and walks around in the darkness; he does not know where he is going, because the darkness has blinded him."*
> 1 John 2:9-11

In the verses preceding it, John sets up this discussion with a series of building blocks:

> *"This is the message we have heard from him and declare to you: God is light; in him there is no darkness at all."*
> 1 John 1:5

We are given insight into who Father is, a startling revelation in its own right:

> *"If we claim to have fellowship with him yet walk in the darkness, we lie and do not live by the truth."*
> Verse 6

There is no wiggle room here. If you want fellowship with Father, spiritual darkness is anathema. Then, John lowers the boom:

> *"But if we walk in the light, as he is in the light, we have fellowship with one another, and the blood of Jesus, his Son, purifies us from all sin."*
> Verse 7

Fellowship with Father necessitates walking in the light of exposure and truth! The supernatural result is not some spiritual high but *fellowship with one another.*

Now the progression is complete. The crux of the matter is at hand:

> *"Anyone who claims to be in the light but hates his brother is still in the darkness."*
> 1 John 2:9

THE QUESTION

Such an eloquently presented theme begs a two-part question: "What is love? And what is hate?" Let's see what the biblical definition of love really is:

*"Love is patient, love is kind. It does not envy,
it does not boast, it is not proud. It is not rude,
it is not self-seeking, it is not easily angered,
it keeps no record of wrongs. Love does not delight
in evil but rejoices with the truth. It always protects,
always trusts, always hopes, always perseveres."*
1 Corinthians 13:4-7

But what of hate? I always ask classes who take my First John course, "How many of you hate somebody?" One or two folks might admit to hating someone but most deny it. Then, while walking out John's thoughts, we come to this question; "What is hate?"

A variety of answers have been offered, mostly characterizing it as something with evil or malevolent intent. Hate is usually reserved for the most extreme circumstances. It is something completely removed from possibility: the students would never hate anyone, and neither would *you.*

We'll see.

In setting the stage can we agree that these things are true?

1. Walking in the light excludes all hatred of the brethren.
2. Such hatred is a form of darkness.
3. There is a glaring inconsistency between professing to know Father while hating your brother.
4. Darkness is incompatible with light.
5. Believing that one's darkness (i.e. hatred) is compatible with light proves that one lives in darkness.
6. Apparently, one may have nominally come into the Kingdom of Light without ever having left the darkness—in which case he is still dwelling in darkness.
7. The brother-hater has made darkness his habitation (see 1 John 2:11).

Therefore, love for the brethren is the barometer of one's fellowship with God.

Fellowship with Father and one another is what the Christian life is all about. Relationship with Father means walking in the light. If you hate your brother, you are not really walking in the light with Father as you think you are. Yours is a relationship of delusion and you live in darkness.

John is often described as the disciple of love, but his love is truly tough love: *"Anyone who hates his brother is a murderer, and you know that no murderer has eternal life in him."* (1 John 3:15).

So, how important is this point? If you hate your brother and don't repent, you aren't on your way to heaven. That's the cold hard truth. Oh, but you don't hate anybody, right?

CONTRASTING LOVE AND HATE

In the biblical pattern there is no neutral ground between love and hate. You either love or you hate. There is no door number three as we have conveniently created with the word "like." "I love him but I don't like him" is the mantra of the brother-hater. In Kingdom life, there is no such thing as "like."

I submit that the opposite of love is hate, both of which can be defined in the simple terms of 1 Corinthians 13:

If love ...	Then hate ...
(is) Patient	(is) Impatient
(is) Kind	(is) Unkind
Does not envy	Envies
Does not boast	Boasts
(is) Not proud	(is) Prideful
(is) Not rude	(is) Rude
(is) Not self-seeking	(is) Selfish
(is) Not easily angered	(is) Quick tempered

126

If love . . .	Then hate . . .
Does not hold grudges	Holds grudges
Rejoices in the truth	Delights in evil
Protects	Exposes to hurt
Trusts	Mistrusts
Hopes	Hopeless
Perseveres Quits	
Never fails Fails	

In one of my classes, I wrote the chart above on a dry erase board while explaining the concept. It took about fifteen minutes to get it all on the board. Then, I just sat down and let them talk.

One woman whispered softly, "I hate my husband." Another said, "I hate just about everybody."

And yet another summed up the response, "We are all brother-haters."

The revelation came for about three hours. I just sat and watched them. The revelation had been assimilated into the students' consciousness.

The next week we took it another step. Racism, sexism, ageism, and denominationalism are all manifestations of hate. Any division (biblical word *"factions,"* see Galatians 5:20; 2 Corinthians 12:20) is **hate**. The Message Bible interprets *"factions"* as *"ugly parodies of community."* True community is only possible through the exercise of love and the elimination of hate.

DEFINING CHRISTIANITY

The New Testament definition of what we call Christianity is founded in the response Jesus gave to those pesky Pharisees:

Hearing that Jesus had silenced the Sadducees, the Pharisees got together. One of them, an expert in the

law, tested him with this question: "Teacher, which is the greatest commandment in the Law?" Jesus replied: "'Love the Lord your God with all your heart and with all your soul and with all your mind.' This is the first and greatest commandment. And the second is like it: 'Love your neighbor as yourself.' All the Law and the Prophets hang on these two commandments."
Matthew 22:34-40

The first part is: *Love the Lord your God*, and the second is equal to the first: *Love your neighbor as yourself.* Everything hangs on these two things: relationship with Father and relationship with one another. Therefore, "sin" it must be understood in the context of this definition as well as the context of First John: ***anything that breaks fellowship is sin.***

Even the Ten Commandments adhere to this standard (Exodus 20).

1. Thou shalt have no other gods before me. (Verse 3)
2. Thou shalt not make unto thee a graven image. (Verse 4)
3. Thou shalt not take the name of Jehovah thy God in vain. (Verse 7)
4. Remember the sabbath day, to keep it holy. (Verse 8)
5. Honor thy father and thy mother. (Verse 12)
6. Thou shalt not kill. (Verse 13)
7. Thou shalt not commit adultery. (Verse 14)
8. Thou shalt not steal. (Verse 15)
9. Thou shalt not bear false witness against thy neighbor. (Verse 16)
10. Thou shalt not covet. (Verse 17)

Every one of these commandments indicates a fellowship killer. The first commandment warns against breaking fellowship with Father. The second warns against replacing fellowship with

Father with something created. Using Father's name in vain is a clear violation of fellowship, as is spending the Sabbath for yourself instead of for Him.

The fifth commandment protects the relationship between parents and children. Killing someone is an obvious fellowship breaker. Committing adultery clearly breaks the intimate relationship between husband and wife. If you steal from someone, then fellowship will surely be destroyed. Fellowship cannot live in an atmosphere of lies. And finally, coveting makes it about their stuff and not about your relationship with them.

All sins are fellowship killers.

The Primary Goal

You can get together with two or three Called Out Ones or with thousands, but the ultimate goal must be paramount: fellowship with Father and fellowship with one another. You can do all the religious stuff, prophesy, preach, or worship, but unless it builds fellowship it is nothing but empty religious tradition.

This is the most difficult admonition you may ever hear: Stop doing church and start being the Saints by digging out hate in your life and filling your being with love for Father and love for one another.

COACH'S TIP

It is time to get off your spiritual couch and get into the eternal game. Don't worry so much about doing; focus upon allowing Father to heal your hurts and changing your ways of thinking. Admit you're a hater, then let transform you into a true lover. Then, you will grow to be a productive citizen of the Promised Land simply by becoming the person of spiritual authority and giftings that you have always known exists within you.

"So that in him we might become
the righteousness of God."
2 Corinthians 5:21

Chapter 13

Coach's Corner

The Obstacles to True Fellowship

"Fellowship? Do you mean to say that I've read this whole book to get to the bottom line of this new adventure and it's just *fellowship*? Isn't that kinda boring, pretty simplistic? I thought there'd be seven keys or five steps or something."

Okay. For all you list people, here are five keys to killing fellowship.

Meetings Kill Fellowship.

Meetings, *all meetings*, are agenda-driven liturgies. Business meetings governed by Robert's Rules of Order are about the liturgy. All traditional church meetings are about the liturgy. The sad fact is, house church meetings often degrade into a liturgy. First, we eat, and then we pray, and then we sing, and then we ... Next week, to make sure there's no accusation of the formulation of a liturgy, we switch it around. Now, we sing, then pray before we eat. We are people of structure and order. We worship our happy little habits as if their very existence conjures God's favor. We strive to find the magic combination that brings the Almighty down from His lofty heights into our mundane existence.

To achieve true fellowship we cannot allow meetings to occur. Meetings are the enemy of fellowship. Inviting someone to a meeting of whatever sort ensures that fellowship will not take place, not really. Oh, we pretend that liturgy is not present, but it sneaks in, like cockroaches in your apartment.

The simplicity of fellowship is found in this: find another Saint or two and worship together, pray together, eat together, study together. It doesn't matter if you fellowship with a family member over a glass of sweet tea in the back yard or when a group of friends get together. The structure kills, so facilitate relational times in which to fellowship with one another and with Father sans structure.

Just hang out!

Liturgy Strangles Fellowship.

Imagine your children approaching you like you approach Father in prayer:

"Father-God, we come into thy presence, Father-God, to seek thy favor, Father-God, in the honor of the car keys, Father-God, so that, Father-God, we mightest knowest the blessings of the movies, Father God, once again on Friday night."

A fellowshipping son or daughter would never approach his/her daddy in such a sterile fashion.

"For you did not receive a spirit that makes you a slave again to fear, but you received the Spirit of **sonship**. *And by him we cry, "Abba, Father." The Spirit himself testifies with our spirit that we are God's children. Now if we are children, then we are heirs—heirs of God and*

co-heirs with Christ, if indeed we share in his sufferings
in order that we may also share in his glory"
Romans 8:15-17 (Bold mine)

This is no simple call to conversational prayer; this is a call to know Daddy deeply (you know very well that the word *Abba* indicates the intimate *daddy*).

Religiosity Is the Enemy of Fellowship.

Religiosity is cookie-cutter Christianity. Rote prayers, liturgies, and agendas are a scourge upon the Called Out Ones. We are held captive by these systems and rigid regularity. Any deviation from the script may be viewed as rebellion.

Spending our time doing silly religious nonsense is a waste of time and counterproductive to the expansion of the Kingdom as well as a satisfying therein.

Religious Tradition Counterfeits Fellowship.

The antidote for institutional mindset is *fellowship*. Religious traditions are clearly the traditions of men. To engage in such things violates the essence of true fellowship. We are held captive by convention. It's time to shed the traditions. The time of: "We've always done it that way!" is quite finished.

He replied, "Isaiah was right when he prophesied about
you hypocrites; as it is written: " 'These people honor
me with their lips, but their hearts are far from me.
They worship me in vain; their teachings are but rules
taught by men.' You have let go of the commands of God
and are holding on to the traditions of men."
And he said to them: "You have a fine way
of setting aside the commands of God
in order to observe your own traditions!"
Mark 7:6-9a

133

False Spiritual Authority Is The Antithesis Of Fellowship.
As noted in the vision of Dragging Out the Dead, the majority of the church crowd is caught up in false spiritual habit: worshipping the liturgy at the expense of fellowship—worshipping the *form* of worship thereby replacing the Giver of life. True life may be found only in innocent abandon in fellowship both with Father and with our spiritual siblings. Any restrictions to that freedom are pure witchcraft. It is time to recognize our complicity in perpetuating:

> ... *having a form of godliness but denying its power.*
> 2 Timothy 3:5

FELLOWSHIP!

And, finally, here are four steps to nurturing fellowship.

Relax!

The "control machine" of the traditional church structure is driven by guilt and condemnation. We have been duped by the notion that Father is more about disapproval than delight. Guilt motivation is the cornerstone of church tradition. Let's just drop it and move on. How? When you feel guilty, quickly confess your sin and celebrate your sonship (of course, daughtership as well):

> *I delight greatly in the Lord; my soul rejoices in my God. For he has clothed me with garments of salvation and arrayed me in a robe of righteousness, as a bridegroom adorns his head like a priest, and as a bride adorns herself with her jewels.*
> Isaiah 61:10

Find Family!

It matters not at all whether you are single or married; search out those through whom the Blood of the Lamb flows. They are your blood kin. Invite them over to your house. Eat together. Laugh, cry, and pray together. Discover Father together.

Kings are only ruled by the King of Kings. Never let another take dominion over you again. Since you were under the dominion of sin and then under the dominion of religious tradition, you are ill-equipped to live like a free person. This is your mission: find family to enjoy!

Find Freedom!

Discover what it means to live free and practice it as long as you live. Stop thinking like a captive! Your mission, should you decide to accept it: find freedom!

Love!

Basic spiritual warfare is against our own hatefulness. Let's discover the divine weapons available for this fight and go about killing hate in every portion of our being. Then, on the journey to and through our Promised Land we will recover, be restored, and learn to live as compassionate kings. The paradox of the Kingdom is we are lovers who fight the fight of faith in love, through love, and because of love.

A FINAL THOUGHT FOR THOSE LEFT BEHIND

If you are a church prisoner who disregarded the warnings contained in the beginning chapters and have read this book anyway, then, I bless you. Remember, this is not intended to encourage you to dig a tunnel under the walls of the institution and escape. Rather, talk to Father for yourself and obey *Him*. The first step on this journey toward maturity is learning that you must hear for *yourself*—whatever the circumstance—and obey **Him not men**. You have read what it takes to escape, but unless you have orders from Father to do so, I think it best you remain where you are for now. However, if I were you, I'd beseech (now there's a church word) Father to let you go.

For those pastors like my friend John Cramer, who stay behind to care for the prisoners, I bless you. Something in these pages may assist you in your work. Few ministries are as close to Father's heart as serving those in prison.

Then the King will say to those on his right,
"Come, you who are blessed by my Father; take your
inheritance, the kingdom prepared for you since the
creation of the world. For I was hungry and
you gave me something to eat, I was thirsty and
you gave me something to drink, I was a stranger and
you invited me in, I needed clothes and you clothed me,
I was sick and you looked after me,
I was in prison and you came to visit me."
Matthew 25:34-36

Coach's Tip

Now that you have escaped your religious prison you must discover what it means to be both a king and a priest in this Kingdom. There are no followers in this Kingdom. There are only leaders. Lead in your home, in your business, and upon the earth. Lead by serving you to others. Don't rule them. Give them you. Care for them; heal them; equip them; and send them out. Stop being a child and be a mature, fellowshipping leader. The rest of us need you!

And hath made us kings and priests unto God and his Father; to him be glory and dominion for ever and ever. Amen.
Revelation 1:6 KJV

ABOUT THE AUTHOR

Tim Mather, Th.D., is the founder and Executive Director of Bear Creek Ranch, a retreat center focusing upon deliverance and wholeness ministry. He has planted and pastored traditional churches until leaving the pastorate to engage the house church movement. He lives in Georgia with his wife Katie surrounded by their four children and many grandchildren. He is the author of *Prophetic Deliverance: The missing Ministry of Jesus in the Church* and *Out of Bondage: Identifying and Breaking Control Spirits in the Church.*

RESOURCES

BOOKS:

Prophetic Deliverance
by Tim Mather

Out of Bondage
by Tim Mather

The Five Wholeness Steps
by Katie Mather

Supernatural Superheroes
by Heather Trim

Visit the Bear Creek Bookstore for more information.
www.BCRcamp.com

More Resources

Audio Teachings:

**Upside Down
Kingdom Weapons**
with Tim Mather

Wholeness JumpStart
with Katie Mather

Made in United States
Troutdale, OR
08/26/2023